FIGHTING GOLIATH

Slaying the Giant of Bipolar Disorder

Jesslyn McCutcheon

©2025 by Jesslyn McCutcheon

Published by hope*books
2217 Matthews Township Pkwy
Suite D302
Matthews, NC 28105
www.hopebooks.com

hope*books is a division of hope*media

Printed in the United States of America

First paperback edition.
Paperback ISBN: 979-8-89185-219-8
Hardcover ISBN: 979-8-89185-189-4
Ebook ISBN: 979-8-89185-224-2
Library of Congress Number: 2025937896

All Scripture quotations, unless otherwise indicated, are taken from the Holy Bible, New International Version®, NIV®. Copyright © 1973, 1978, 1984, 2011 by Biblica, Inc.™ Used by permission of Zondervan. All rights reserved worldwide. www.zondervan.com The "NIV" and "New International Version" are trademarks registered in the United States Patent and Trademark Office by Biblica, Inc.™

hope*books
hopebooks.com

Because the world needs your hope-filled words now more than ever

Jesslyn's McCutcheon's *Fighting Goliath: Slaying the Giant of Bipolar Disorder* transforms the psyche, something I've never experienced before from a book-reading it as not so much a vicarious experience as it is a new lived experience, on that gives us strength to surrender, full-armed, to the Great Physician, even if we must become David again and again.

—**Mary Hughes Lee**
Founder of the Sid Lee Memorial Mental Health
Association (Sid's House), Walnut Cove, NC

I found *Fighting Goliath: Slaying the Giant of Bipolar Disorder* to be refreshingly raw–Jesslyn didn't hold back on the actual experience of discovering your mental illness and how confusing and disheartening that process can be. Jesslyn highlighted the impact of mental illness on the family and how everyone goes through that together (her family journal entries and letters were a lovely and heartbreaking touch). Finally, her exploration of faith will speak to a lot of followers of Christ who have gone through the same journey and had trouble reconciling the faith of their youth with their experiences with a mental health condition. It was a solid read.

—**Amy L. Brundle, M. Div.**
Marketing and Communications Manager
at NAMI North Carolina

Fighting Goliath is a faith-filled guide for anyone supporting a loved one battling mental illness or life's toughest challenges. Jesslyn shares her journey of confronting bipolar disorder and finding restoration through surrender to God's plan with raw honesty and deep spiritual insight. This book provides practical tools, wisdom, and hope, showing how to overcome even the darkest moments. It's a lifeline for families and friends who feel helpless, offering understanding and the reassurance that no battle is too great when fought with God's strength. A powerful testimony of resilience and faith, this book inspires readers to face their giants with courage, trust, and the promise of victory in Christ.

—Kim Mosiman
Author of *Reflections of Joy* and Christian Wellness Coach

Jesslyn McCutcheon has been a valuable friend and ally to our church and my ministry in the area of mental health. I am very thankful she is tackling such an important challenge that impacts so many, including those we love or ourselves personally. This is a great resource that brings hope and understanding in the midst of the struggle from one who knows firsthand.

—Pastor Tom Hypes
The Shepherd's Fellowship, Marion, OH

As a survivor of a nervous breakdown and having battled depression and anxiety, I'm so grateful that Jesslyn wrote this amazing book. She beautifully weaves Scripture throughout her story and offers insight and encouragement through trusting Jesus, praying, meditating on His Word, doctors, medication, counseling, and all the many things available to those dealing with mental illness. Her book also sheds light on the great depth of tragedy in the stigma associated with mental illness.

—Sandy Milner
Friend & Sister-in-Christ, First Baptist King

In her book, *Fighting Goliath: Slaying the Giant of Bipolar Disorder*, Jesslyn McCutcheon courageously dares to pull back the curtain behind which her mental illness held her prisoner for many years. With raw honesty and transparency, she shares the intimate details of the inner turmoil she suffered at the hands of a giant too big for her to wage war against on her own. Enter Jesus…and hope. From the heart of a survivor, Jesslyn shares the victory she experienced as she fought her battle against mental illness with not only professional treatment, but with a faith that moves mountains—and slays giants. As someone who ministers to women with loved ones who struggle with addiction and mental health issues, as well as having an adult child of my own who battles mental illness, I am grateful to come alongside Jesslyn to support her in this important work she is doing to spread the message of hope to those who are courageously fighting their own Giants.

—Dawn R. Ward
Founder of The Faith to Flourish and author of *From Guilt To Grace: Hope and Healing for Christian Moms of Addicted Children*

I wholeheartedly endorse this work by Jesslyn McCutcheon, *Fighting Goliath*. According to the National Institute of Mental Health, approximately 23.1% of adults struggle with mental illness. I, too, struggle with mental health, and find this book to be of immense value for the battle at hand. Jesslyn taps into a powerful tool to regain control of your life that is usually neglected by modern Psychology: Heart transformation by the gracious power of the almighty God.

—Pastor Stephen Mannion
Clarence Global Methodist Church and host of
The Jesus Agenda Podcast

Fighting Goliath is a powerful, captivating, and mind-opening story about the effects of negative mental health. Jesslyn is very open and transparent about all that she has been through, her faith, and her beliefs in God. He is not done with Jesslyn, but is using her in a mighty way to help those who are or have been dealing with mental health issues.

—Brian Tucker
Director of Christian Mix Media International

In Jesslyn's book, *Fighting Goliath*, she skillfully taps the shoulder of those suffering with mental illness and gently says to them: "I get it. I have given your suffering words that others will understand on your behalf. I can also point you to the hope of healing that I found through Jesus and the people and treatments He lovingly brought into my life." *Fighting Goliath* is what you get when you merge a testimony of God's grace with an informative Bible-centered book about mental illness written by an expert. In the past I too suffered from bouts of mental illness and this book would have been very comforting for me in that season of darkness.

—**Charles Wagner**
Executive Director of Gramazin Inc.

This book is a must read. Jesslyn tells all, putting her life and struggles out there that many of us hide everyday. This book will help break the stigma of mental illness and will help to give you a voice, a family member, or a friend. Her testimony will change the way you view mental health. I like how she bares all and doesn't hold back. Most of all I love how she shares that she knew she couldn't beat this alone. She needs to trust God and His process.

—**Lorraine Childs**
Founder of Lending My Voice

Fighting Goliath is a raw and honest journey through the daily struggles of living with bipolar disorder. With courage and authenticity, Jesslyn leads the way to freedom and truth, having walked this path herself. This book unlocks the secrets and shame of those with mental illness and brings healing and hope to those tender places. At the same time, it fosters deeper compassion and understanding for those who do not personally experience mental illness, equipping them to support and love more fully. When you read the last word, you will be reminded that God is working, always working, to bring beauty out of our broken stories.

—**Lea Turner**
Speaker, coach, and author of *The Freedom to Feel:
Finding God in Grief and Trauma*

DISCLAIMER

PLEASE NOTE THAT THIS BOOK SHOULD NOT BE CONSID-
ERED AS A SUBSTITUTE AT ANY TIME FOR PROFESSIONAL
MEDICAL CARE TREATMENT OR DIAGNOSIS, PROFESSIONAL
MENTAL HEALTH COUNSELING, OR SPIRITUAL GUIDANCE
FOR YOUR INDIVIDUAL CIRCUMSTANCES. THE INTENTION
BEHIND THIS BOOK IS TO PROVIDE HOPE TO THE HOPELESS
WHEN IT COMES TO LIVING WITH BIPOLAR DISORDER OR
ANY MENTAL HEALTH CONDITION.

To protect the privacy of those mentioned in this book, names have
been changed or certain story details excluded when necessary.

PLEASE BE AWARE

This book contains material regarding suicidal ideation and a suicide
attempt. If at any time you find yourself triggered or distressed by
this book please reach out for help. A list of helpful organizations is
available in the Resources section of the book.

IN MEMORY

To my father Kenneth Wayne Geras
The man who taught me to stand firm in my faith—
to witness the deliverance that only Christ can bring.
May 30, 1946–July 31, 2024

DEDICATION

To the One who saved my soul, The Hero of the story, the Alpha and Omega, Jesus Christ my Savior.

To my husband Jason Paul McCutcheon—God designed you for me. This book would not have been possible without your support. You are my calm in the chaos. My biggest cheerleader. You are the definition of what it means to love another.

To my mother Cheryl Lea Geras—you are the strongest woman that I know. You have given me life not once, but a number of times.

To my girls—Isabella, Selah, and Abigail—there is no greater joy than to be your mom.

ACKNOWLEDGEMENTS

To my husband and children:
I want to express my deepest gratitude to my incredible husband and children for their unwavering support and patience. Thank you for allowing me the time, space, and encouragement to write this book. Your understanding and love made this book possible. I am forever grateful.

To my Fighting Goliath for Mental Illness family:
My ministry is the passion of my heart, and I am so grateful for each of you. Thank you for being part of this community and for supporting one another—whether emotionally, practically, or through shared resources and knowledge. We are united by a common goal: to reduce stigma, raise awareness, and foster understanding about mental health. We truly 'get' one another, and my cup overflows with gratitude for our shared connection.

To my publishing family:
I discovered hope*books Publishing while recovering from my third major neck surgery. From the beginning, I felt an undeniable sense that this would be the perfect home for my hope-filled words. I am deeply thankful for the leadership and servant-hearted vision of Brian Dixon, the founder of hope*books. A special thank you to my Developmental Editor, Abby McDonald, whose wisdom and expert guidance on my manuscript were invaluable. I am also grateful to my Copy Assistant for her meticulous attention to detail, addressing grammatical errors and offering thoughtful notes. To Hope Dover and the rest of the hope*books team, thank you for all the efforts made in making this book a reality and for the education and support that you have provided to turn me from a writer to an author. To the

community of authors and friendships made, what a beautiful gift each of you has given me! May God bless you abundantly and grant favor to your ministries as you continue serving others.

To all the BETA readers:
Your comments and suggestions made my book better. Thank you for your invaluable time and your willingness to come alongside me and support this project.

To the book endorsers:
I will forever cherish your heartfelt words of kindness. Thank you for your belief and support for *Fighting Goliath: Slaying the Giant of Bipolar Disorder*.

To my book launch managers:
Kim Mosiman and Lea Turner with Writer-to-Writer: a dynamic duo and gifted authors who are dedicated to helping fellow authors suc-ceed in the publishing world. I could not have launched my book without their support. They walked alongside me every step of the way. Thank you both!

To my Church Family at First Baptist King (FBK):
I am deeply grateful for my church family. Your prayers, encourage-ment, and constant reminders that we are never alone have provided great comfort. To my sisters-in-Christ, my Sunday school class, and the Ladies' Prayer Group—thank you for our beautiful and treasured bond. The support has been irreplaceable to the leadership and dea-con families who have stood with us through joyful and challenging times. Thank you all for exemplifying what it truly means to be the body of Christ.

To my mother:
Your love, strength, and constant care throughout these 25 years have been my greatest comfort and source of strength. I am forever grateful for your presence, and I could not have made it through without you by my side.

To my brothers:
Jason and Jordan, you have always been there from the beginning of this journey. I love you both deeply and dearly.

To family and friends:
Thank you for your unwavering support throughout my journey and for standing by me. Your patience and understanding have been the foundation of my healing, and I am profoundly grateful. Your presence and encouragement have been a constant source of strength. I am truly blessed to have you in my life.

To the mental health professionals:
Thank you for your tireless efforts and the work that you do in the mental health field. I am deeply grateful to everyone who has played and continues to play a vital role in my journey.

CONTENTS

INTRODUCTION

"The stone sank into his forehead, and he fell
facedown on the ground."
—1 Samuel 17:49

Giant steps shake the earth—legs like tree trunks, fists like stone. No one expects you to stand a chance. You are the underdog standing in front of a 9'9" Philistine giant warrior with your five smooth stones and a stick. You are made fun of, cursed, threatened, and mocked. David said to the Philistine:

> You come against me with a sword and spear and javelin, but I come against you in the name of the Lord Almighty, the God of the armies of Israel, whom you have defied. This day the Lord will deliver you into my hands, and I'll strike you down and cut off your head. This very day I will give the carcasses of the Philistine army to the birds and the wild animals, and the whole world will know that there is a God in Israel. All those gathered here will know that it is not by sword or spear that the Lord saves; for the battle is the Lord's, and he will give all of you into our hands (1 Samuel 17:45-47).

This book was not easy to write. One that I never anticipated writing. To share my story is only by the grace of God. I was six feet under. Would I ever achieve the victory of rising from my grave and returning to existence? Was I going to rise from the rubble and look my giant straight in the eyes? *Fighting Goliath* is a true story of slaying the biggest giant of my life–living with bipolar disorder. Giants can be anything that seeks to destroy or diminish the life God desires and intended for us from the beginning. The journey we will take together combines personal stories, practical advice, and spiritual guidance. This book is for any person, family member, friend, colleague, mental health professional, or advocate who has been affected by bipolar disorder or a mental health condition.

Every year, millions look to the internet for answers to their deepest hurts and struggles. According to the 2023 *United States National Survey on Drug Use and Health*, 59.0% (or 167.2 million people) Americans ages 12 and older used tobacco products, vaped nicotine, used alcohol, or used an illicit drug in the past month.[1] The CDC states that suicide is one of the leading causes of death in the United States. Over 49,000 people died by suicide in 2022.[2] That is one death every 11 minutes after wrestling with worthlessness, fear, anxiety, and hopelessness. Each of these individuals is hurting and longing to be understood, have hope, and be heard.

Only a small circle of family and friends knew the invisible war and the giant my family and I were facing. The ongoing battle would continue to plague me and our family for the rest of our lives. We were unprepared for this fight. What do you do when out-of-nowhere circumstances happen in your life that you didn't see coming? How do you keep pressing ahead? What do you do when the smoke, clouds, and darkness suffocate? When the walls are closing in on you? What do you do when you feel like you cannot go on anymore, and the lie comes from the pit of despair you don't even want to live? The questions keep marching on into infinity until you get to the real business. What does it mean to surrender your giant to God? Satan will tempt Christians with his power. Amid all your trouble, can you still find the goodness of God? The earth groans under the weight of all your sins.

The question we need to ask is, are you ready to start listening

---

1 Substance Abuse and Mental Health Services Administration (SAMHSA). *United States National Survey on Drug Use and Health (NSDUH)*. 2023, https://www.samhsa.gov/data/sites/default/files/NSDUH%202023%20Annual%20Release/2023-nsduh-main-highlights.pdf.
2 Centers for Disease Control and Prevention (CDC), *Suicide Data and Statistics*, 2024, https://www.cdc.gov/suicide/facts/data.html.

to the voice of God rather than your own? You are not capable of fighting this battle all alone. It is time to start running towards your giant head-on, looking him straight in the eyes with the confidence that God is the Way Maker, the Lord of Lords, our Chief Cornerstone. Believe that no weapon formed against you shall prosper (Isaiah 54:17). Stop running in the other direction. His love can overcome the darkness in this world and heal your brokenness. We need to stop pondering about what the world says and start thinking about what He can do. He will give you the provision.

I was diagnosed with Bipolar I Disorder at the age of 26. These were unwanted circumstances that I did not want any part of. There was no amount of wishing it or praying it away. It took years before receiving the proper diagnosis. Did I ever imagine, in my wildest dreams, I would be writing a book about living with an acute mental illness? I wrote this book from the perspective of lived experience. The information provided comes from years of gut-wrenching heartache and pain, trying to navigate how one is to live with bipolar disorder, a chronic illness that has no cure.

However, on the other hand, you will find great trials and tribulations we faced that only a big king, the King of Kings, could resolve. In the end, you will see a story of redemption by surrendering to trust in the armies of the living God. His resurrection turned me right side up after I was once turned upside down. You will see a story about a woman who was asking all the wrong questions and about a God who was with her in the waiting. A story that I can now boldly and confidently share and declare to others that He is always there in your waiting and suffering.

In my failures, Jesus prepared me with the foundation to transform my life. He is still working when all we hear is silence. We serve a God who provides wisdom to face your worst enemies day in and day out. You will find that the world we live in today does not have the final say. It is not over until God says it is over. He is the Alpha and the Omega. No one is an exception when it comes to obeying God. No amount of money, your race, the house you live in, the car you drive, or what kind of business you may own matters. What matters is saying '*yes*' to God.

I had to learn to defeat the mind games the devil played once and for all, or my mind and the bondage maker of despair were going to continue to manage me and my mind. Often, we lack the tools needed to succeed because the pain is unfathomable to manage and cuts too deep. I lost sight of trying to see the good in anything I had to face to take care of myself. I had to learn to stand on His promises confidently, knowing that I would prevail when I did. And you will prevail, too! I had to escape the silence, secrecy, shame, and stigma. I had to learn to guard my heart with His rules, not mine. I had to grasp all over again what faith is and is not. Faith, my friends, is not living your life in constant fear. Faith is to stop thinking about what you can do and start thinking about what He can. We wonder why we stay in the wilderness alone for so long. Often, if truth be told, it is because we do not make the best decisions when we are desperate. You must have the eyes of faith.

What matters is people, community, and belief that you no longer have to carry the pain of living with the circumstances in your life that are trying to kill and destroy you. I could continue to stay quiet, or I could be who God created me to be and go out and slay the biggest giant of my life under His protection, knowing that I would never fail. You can only win this fierce battle with God. You cannot be afraid. You have to keep moving forward and not by yourself. I have, by His divine grace and mercy, defied many of the limited assumptions people perceive mental illness to be. I know that if all I continued to listen to were Satan's lies, to live under the shadow of my illness, I was never going to reach that mountaintop or be set free. It took me over two decades to fully surrender, and when I did, my calling, my purpose, hit me like the stone that went straight into Goliath's forehead.

Trust me, if there is adversity in your life, it is for a greater purpose. The apostle Paul stated: "Then we will no longer be infants, tossed back and forth by the waves, and blown here and there by every wind of teaching and by the cunning and craftiness of people in their

4

deceitful scheming. Instead, speaking the truth in love, we will grow to become in every respect the mature body of him who is the head, that is, Christ" (Ephesians 4:14-15). Your spiritual growth and maturity will depend on how you respond every time. I needed wisdom and a complete transformation—a heart transformation. Once I fully surrendered my whole heart to God, he molded me and continues to mold me into a beautiful tapestry of redemption.

God knows how to get our attention. When our lives are falling apart, you wonder, *Where is He? Does God even care?* Your life may feel like it is unraveling, and God may seem distant, but even then, He is at work. Right when you think your breakthrough is near, another stone is thrown. God may be silent, but He is never still. He wants you to rely on Him. By not fully trusting, you continue to cheat yourself out of what He wants us to accomplish for His glory. God has already decreed His will for your life.

Living with a mental illness is a lifelong journey. It is not a linear process. There will not be a quick fix or a snap out of it solution. And there never will be—this reflects a lack of misunderstanding about mental health conditions. Living with bipolar disorder is complex, and how I manage to stay healthy is by finding that balance between what is medically necessary to take care of my illness and my faith. What I do know is that the Lord Jehovah is my strength and my song. "Surely God is my salvation; I will trust and not be afraid. The Lord, the Lord himself, is my strength and my defense; he has become my salvation" (Isaiah 12:2). My hope for you is to know that whatever giant you may be facing in your life, it is not bigger than Jesus Christ. The fire and passion ignited in my soul completely changed my life. Through my brokenness and weakness, He has given me the ability, courage, empowerment, and this supernatural boldness to now share my story with you. This book would never have been the case if I was disconnected from the One in a class all by Himself. You have to know how to fight to survive. It is not our job to figure out our life. It is our assignment to trust the only Messiah who can. After you finish reading *Fighting Goliath*, you will find that by turning your focus toward the Provider, through the power of Christ, your giants can fall.

CHAPTER 1

SHEOL

*"Slowly the darkness began to weave its way into my mind, and
before long I was hopelessly out of control."*
—Kay Redfied Jamison[3]

The year was 1999, and it felt like my world was ending. I walked into work looking like I had stepped out of a windstorm—same clothes, unwashed, my hair barely tamed. My outward appearance screamed to all that something was wrong. Every part of me looked like I had just rolled out of bed. I felt the many eyes of my colleagues watching as I made my way to my cubicle to put my things down. Anxiety tightened its grip as I walked, every step amplifying the weight in my chest. A sense of nervousness, restlessness, and panic started to take over. My heart began to pound fast, and the anxiety that was building screamed. My hands trembled. I felt a panic attack brewing.

Not a single person spoke—everyone only stared. It felt like one of those Lifetime movies where the main character is on the verge of breaking, with everyone around her just waiting for her to crash and burn. My boss called me into his office before I could settle my things. I knew what he would say; everyone did. He gestured to the chair across from him and told me to have a seat. He softly and carefully said, "I have noticed that you have not been yourself lately, and there has been a noticeable decline in your appearance. Is everything alright?"

What was I supposed to say? I managed to nod as if I was agreeing with him, but on the inside, I was crumbling. I knew that I was on the

---

3 Jamison, Kay Redfield. *An Unquiet Mind*, Vintage Books, 1995, p. 79.

verge of a complete breakdown. I gathered my things, fought the dam of tears, and headed for the door, feeling the weight of side glances and whispers as I walked out. That day was a pivotal turning point for me. I did not look back—not one time.

In a month, my whole countenance had changed. The inner turmoil that I was fighting kept me away from everyone. I shut down and did not want to interact with anyone—not my friends, boyfriend, or even my family, could break the vicious cycle of decline. I talked to no one. Isolating myself felt safe; it quieted the noise in my head by sleeping. My days consisted of sleeping all day. For the times I did drag myself out of the bed, I would start to pick at my skin obsessively for hours. Picking at my skin became an endless ritual, my fingers searching and digging as if I could pull the darkness from beneath my skin. Hours would slip away, swallowed by the mirror's unrelenting glare.

Did you know that there are over 20,000 pores on your face alone? I recognize each pore intimately, desperately looking to draw the madness out of the inside of my brain. Picking at my skin became my outlet. What started as a minor compulsion spiraled into an obsession, swallowing whole hours of my day and my night as the lights continued to dim—until finally, everything faded to quiet, endless darkness.

I felt like I had become a worthless person. I felt useless, wretched, and ugly–this was not life. I did not know what this was. I was a prisoner sitting in my jail cell that I could not escape. I was enduring both physical and psychological torture. I was consumed by darkness, with Satan whispering in my ear, telling me every single day that I was too weak to pull myself out. He urged me to keep digging into my skin, making myself bleed.

The Father of Lies will try to convince you that you will never be able to rise above the rubble. He will slither around you like a snake and make you feel like you are all alone. "Be alert and of sober mind. Your enemy the devil prowls around you like a roaring lion seeking someone to devour. Resist him, standing firm in the faith, because you know that the family of believers throughout the world is undergoing the same kind of sufferings" (1 Peter 5:8-9). He will tempt you, test you, and tell you that you have become too far gone and not even God can save you this time. In the book of Matthew, we learn about Jesus' temptation in the wilderness:

> Then Jesus was led by the Spirit into the wilderness to be tempted by the devil. After fasting forty days and forty nights, he was hungry. The tempter came to him and said, "If you are the Son of God, tell these stones to become bread." Jesus answered, "It is written: 'Man shall not live on bread alone, but on every word that comes from the mouth of God.'" Then, the devil took him to the holy city and had him stand on the temple's highest point. "If you are the Son of God," he said, "throw yourself down. For it is written: '"He will command his angels concerning you, and they will lift you up in their hands, so that you will not strike your foot against a stone.'" Jesus answered him, "It is also written: 'Do not put the Lord your God to the test.'" Again, the devil took him to a very high mountain and showed him all the kingdoms of the world and their splendor. "All this I will give you," he said, "if you will bow down and worship me." Jesus said to him, "Away from me, Satan! For it is written: 'Worship the Lord your God, and serve him only.'" Then the devil left him, and angels came and attended him (Matthew 4:1-11).

The first temptation was turning stones into bread, implying that Jesus should use His power for His benefit. The second temptation was Jesus throwing Himself down from the temple. Jesus responded by quoting Deuteronomy 6:16, which says, "Do not put the Lord your God to the test." In the third temptation, once again, Jesus chooses obedience to His Father's plan over the demands of this world. There is power in knowing His words and watching the enemy flee.

The lie the enemy relentlessly tried to convince me of was that I was sinking and the waters were too deep for me to survive. He was not moving away from me—he was moving wickedly closer. A war was waging within, and the intrusive thoughts consumed and plagued my mind. He was trying to convince me that my last breath was coming and every piece of me was decaying. It felt like it was just a matter of time. Scared and confused, I did not know if God was hearing my cries for help from the dark prison that now appeared to be my home. The devil was a master at making me think it would be better if I had disappeared permanently. I felt myself entering the kingdom of Satan and feeling how much he wanted me to suffer. Satan is the king of adversity. He wanted me to question my faith. Little by little, he was winning, chipping pieces of my faith away. Why was this happening? What had I done so wrong to deserve this? I felt myself heading into a spiritual tailspin. The devil was trying his best to shatter my faith.

I was skin and bones, rail thin, weighing 96 pounds at 5'6". I craved the darkness; the blinds stayed closed during the day as if the light reminded me of the world I no longer wanted to be a part of. I stayed hidden away in my self-destructing cage, an animal that did not want to be a part of the world. I was alive. There was breath in my lungs, but I was slowly fading away. My spirit withered in the silence. No one saw me—I had become a ghost, a shadow of my former self. I had no idea who this was–I saw a stranger I no longer recognized. Trapped in a cycle of extreme sadness and unexplained crying spells, it felt as if all the light and hope had depleted from me, leaving nothing but a hollow shell.

Abby, my roommate and one of my best friends from college, was scared. She did not know what lay ahead or if I would be there the next day.

Journal, June 2000

I look in the mirror and do not know who that person is looking back at me. I isolate myself from everyone. I withdraw from family and friends. I do not smile anymore. I hear nothing. My life brings overwhelming sadness–I am empty. I feel worthless. I have nothing left–nothing. Satan reigns victorious. The enemy's hateful arrows hit me over and over again. God, who am I? Where are You?

Why is it that, in our desperation to hear from God, He often remains silent? We ask countless questions: *Where are You, God? Do You even see me? What have I done to deserve this? Why do You remain silent?* Please, say something—anything! After weeks, months, and even years drag on, our faith begins to go dry. We wonder: *Is He abandoning me? What is the purpose that lies behind all this pain? Why am I left to navigate this hurt, this illness, this loss of a loved one, this divorce, all on my own? Why are there no answers? What are we to do in the silence?*

In times of doubt and frustration, it can feel as if pain surrounds you. Yet even in your darkest moments, remember that He is present; He has not abandoned you. Silence does not mean He is inactive; God is always working for our good, even when it is hard to see through the fog of suffering. We may feel disconnected from the rest of the world, engulfed in the flames of pain– feeling numb, afraid, unhappy, irritable, and paranoid thinking, but you have to know that He is there. He has not just up and quit on you. Adversity can damage our faith, which I know all too well. I have battled the forces of darkness more times than I can count. Even when silence surrounds you, and your world seems stone cold, God is never still. He is constantly working for our good. Do not let the lies play on repeat in your mind. Do not give the kingdom of Satan the upper hand. I had felt forgotten, struggling to understand why my life had changed drastically. I was desperately seeking how to navigate the pain. I did not understand, and nothing made sense to me. Everywhere I turned, I was not hearing the voice of God–not even a whisper. I felt abandoned. Have you ever felt abandoned?

"But if I go to the east, he is not there; if I go to the west, I do not find him. When he is at work in the north, I do not see him; when he turns to the south, I catch no glimpse of him" (Job 23:8-9). The difference between Job and me was that I could not see how God would use any of this darkness for my good or anyone. I felt like I was being punished and tortured. Job is teaching us that even when we cannot see in our moments of suffering, our Sovereign God is still at work. He is working in ways we cannot see.

I do not remember my parents coming to get me; I had not initiated any contact. Abby had orchestrated everything behind the scenes, calling them after she reached her breaking point of watching me wither away. The day my parents arrived at our apartment was a blur. I do not recall getting into a car, putting on shoes, or conversing. I was merely existing, devoid of the ability to care about anything. My thoughts spiraled, consumed by a relentless urge to escape life itself. The darkness haunted me, and my mind raced uncontrollably, refusing to quiet down. Sleep became my only refuge, the only way to silence the chaos storming in my head. The devil worked tirelessly to wear me down with discouragement, confusion, guilt, strife, fear, and depression. He wanted me to surrender. My thoughts would paralyze me—and I was no longer functioning. The weight of depression was debilitating, and anxiety suffocated my soul. The darkness felt insurmountable, the valley too deep, the walls closing in. This pit—my open grave—seemed to have no exit, leaving me uncertain if I would ever find the strength to crawl back out. For the first time in my life, I felt hopeless.

The story of Joseph, primarily found in Genesis chapters 37-50, tells us that he dealt with adversity alone. Joseph was the eleventh son of Jacob and the firstborn of his wife, Rachel. Joseph was the favorite and was given a coat of many colors by his father, which made all his brothers jealous. The jealousy within the brothers continued to deepen when Joseph had dreams that one day he would rule over all of them. Out of rage and jealousy, Joseph was unexpectedly thrown into a pit, like me, not knowing if his exit would come. His brothers grabbed him, stripped him of the robe his father had passed down to him, and out of nowhere, found himself dumped into a dry well. His brothers wanted him gone. They hated Joseph and his dreams. They wanted him to disappear because his brothers saw that their father loved and favored Joseph more than any of them.

Satan wanted me to disappear just like Joseph's twelve brothers. He was tempting me to think this way. I felt as if I was sent to this dungeon cell to rot—and for what? What did I do so wrong to deserve this? It did not seem fair. In Joseph's journey, the Lord never left or forgot him. Joseph was sold into slavery to the Ishmaelites by his brothers and, next, sold to Potiphar, the captain of Pharaoh's body-guard, as his slave. Joseph was a hard worker. For years, he worked as an enslaved person for Potiphar. He eventually found himself seduced by Potiphar's wife.

"His master's wife looked with desire at Joseph, and she said, 'Lie with me'" (Genesis 39:7). When Joseph refused her, this upset her, and she became angry and gave false testimony that Joseph tried to rape her. His captors cast Joseph into the dark prison once again. After 13 years of trials and misery, something good finally happened. "When two full years had passed, Pharaoh had a dream" (Genesis 41:1). "In the morning his mind was troubled, so he sent for all the magicians and wise men of Egypt. Pharaoh told them his dreams, but no one could interpret them for him" (Genesis 41:8). My faith wavered. However, Joseph's faith remained strong. Joseph was falsely accused and thrown into prison for a crime he did not commit. One of Pharaoh's officials, the cupbearer, remembered Joseph could inter-pret dreams, so Pharaoh would summon him. With the help of God, Joseph predicted the dream, and Pharaoh made him second-in-com-mand over all of Egypt. Despite his adversity, Joseph remained faith-ful to God when everything around him looked hopeless.

The decision to try and end my life was impulsive. All the warn-ing signs had been building over this course of time. I felt empty, hopeless, trapped—as if there was no escape. I could not find my way through the fog. I was anxious and extremely sad. The emotional pain was unbearable. I could not see past the cycle of the state of severe de-pression that I was in. The hopelessness was cruel—I felt like I could no longer breathe. I did not bother asking for help. I believed there was no help left to give. My decision was sudden. I was fearless, and I said nothing to anyone. My flesh was telling me this was the end. I lost control and made the unthinkable suicide attempt. The battle in my mind was only beginning.

This journal entry was recorded by my mom the night of my suicide attempt:

Journal, June 2000

The ambulance took her away, tubes down her throat. She was in another world—not a part of our lives. We were losing our daughter. Right before our very eyes.

When someone is admitted to the emergency room for a suicide attempt, a mental health professional will evaluate the person's physical and emotional health. The evaluation is assessing your suicide risk to determine the level of care that you need. I could hardly say that I was not suicidal with the evidence of black charcoal covering the front of my clothes. The medical personnel tried to ask me many questions. It seemed like the questions would never end. I gave short responses to answer *yes* or *no*. What was the point? You may be asked the following questions:

- What symptoms are you having?
- Have you ever been treated for mental health before?
- Does anyone in your family have a history of mental health?
- Did you want to die?
- Have you ever received medical/psychiatric treatment before?

I would come to understand that mental illness ran on my father's side of the family. There was a strong genetic component. Genetic and environmental risks travel in families, just like it does for cancer and diabetes–this was not something anyone had done. It came from something transpiring within my brain. Looking back, I remember that when we visited my grandmother as children, she would rest a lot. She rarely left her bedroom for long periods. She would never stay to visit very long–she had to go back and lie down to rest again. My mother recounted a visit my grandparents made while we were living in Longview, Texas. I was in third grade. My mom was cleaning the kitchen floor one day while my grandmother watched intensely from the sofa in the other room. She became upset, convinced that the cleaning solution that my mom was using to clean the floor would poison us all.

Many times during my parents' marriage, they often visited my grandmother when she needed hospitalization for further care. During some of those visits, she barely spoke, staring blankly at the walls, seemingly oblivious to everything around her. If anyone tried to ask her a question, she would not respond, as though she could not even hear them.

I remember once as a family driving through a car wash when my grandmother, gripped with terror, fear, and paranoia, tried to open the door to escape, even as the car was still moving through the machinery. My father's brother also battled with his mental health challenges but chose not to pursue the treatment that he needed.

In the ER, a kind lady sat outside my room to watch over me. She called me "*baby*" and *"honey."* She asked if she could get me anything to drink and said she would pray for my healing. That day, I was overwhelmed by a paranoid feeling that everyone who walked past my room and saw the woman sitting by my door knew why I was there.

It was like there was a neon blinking sign outside my room that said, *"She just attempted suicide."* My family stayed with me until transport came and got me hours later. My parents knew I was terrified, and they were too. I had an overall look of horror—this was uncharted territory, and none of us knew how to navigate this new journey.

That day, I lost everything. They handed me a set of dull green scrubs and a pair of hideous dark purple hospital safety socks designed to prevent slipping. Even now, the sight of these socks makes my stomach churn. They took my shoes with the laces, citing safety precautions. The last thing they took was the cross hanging around my neck that I never took off. My mother gave it to me as a reminder that, even on the loneliest days, Jesus was still with me. They reassured me that they would keep it in a safe place until discharged, but the ache of losing that necklace intensified the current circumstances.

The trip from the ER to the behavioral health unit was embarrassing and humiliating. A hospital security officer and someone from the behavioral health team escorted me to the floor. Anyone we passed in the hallway stared, just like my coworkers had. With a security officer walking beside me, I knew from the looks that they were wondering what I had done. I felt like I had committed some awful crime—only adding to what I had already faced. What crime did I commit? Being mentally sick? Why should being mentally ill be treated any differently than being physically ill? My head fell in shame until we got to the psychiatric unit, where they buzzed me in—the heavy door locked and shut behind me. They gave me a code to share with my parents if they wanted to call me. The only way to communicate with me was if they had that code. Everything around me looked drab and colorless. There were no knobs on the doors and no hooks on the walls. The room was bare. How are you supposed to feel any better in an environment like this? The room contained a wooden single bed frame with a thin mattress that was far from comfortable—the beds were never meant to be. There are no sharp objects in the room or mirrors. They placed the television screen behind a piece of plexiglass. The lights in the room were bright. They provided 24/7 care, checking on you every 15 minutes. That completely irritated and annoyed me.

Each morning, the staff took vital signs at various times. They expected participation at breakfast, lunch, and dinner, as well as during various therapy sessions held throughout the day. There is a day center room where patients can sit, watch television, and interact with others in the unit. All I wanted was to go back home. The length of stay and discharge date varied for each patient. I kept to myself, avoiding sessions and refusing to participate, hoping they would leave me alone.

They began treating me for Major Depressive Disorder (MDD), a mood disorder that affects the entire body, including thoughts and emotions. Depression arises from an imbalance of neurotransmitters, including serotonin, norepinephrine, and dopamine. It often runs in families and can be triggered by life events or certain illnesses. I experienced all the main symptoms:

- Pervasive sadness, emptiness, and hopelessness.
- Loss of interest in nearly all activities.
- Changes in appetite and weight.
- Changes in sleep.
- Physical aches and pains.
- Lack of concentration.
- Loss of energy.
- Recurring thoughts of death and suicide.

The weight of depression feels like carrying heavy rocks in a backpack that pulls you down, as if shackles were attached to your ankles, making even simple movements a struggle. During my hospitalization, I was started on an antidepressant and informed that it might take four to six weeks for the medication to take full effect.

For a minute, imagine looking around and visualizing everything, everyone moving, yet you cannot see or feel it. The world continues to move, but you are standing still. On the outside, everything looks fine; you are still alive, but on the inside, you feel all alone and numb. According to HealthCentral, MDD is more than just feeling sad, experiencing grief, or a draining of energy. Those feelings are valid; like most feelings, they will eventually pass. MDD is often a debilitating mental illness that presents as a cluster of depressive symptoms. For most people, clinical depression will not go away on its own, and you cannot *just snap out of it*. While melancholy and exhaustion are part of depression, there are other symptoms to look for, including losing interest in things you once enjoyed, trouble sleeping, sudden crying spells, withdrawing from others, hopelessness, thoughts of self-harm or suicide, and more.[4]

Many people with clinical depression do their best to conceal symptoms from the people surrounding them. They may feel vulnerable and embarrassed for showing weakness or worry that their friends and colleagues might judge or ghost them. Remember: MDD is not a

---

4 Devash, Meirav. "Major Depressive Disorder (Unipolar Depression)." *HealthCentral*, 5 Apr. 2024, www.healthcentral.com/condition/major-depressive-disorder.

negative attitude, a character flaw, or a sign of weakness. Some people with depression cannot recognize it in themselves. The symptoms can pop up gradually, and before you know it, you have not been to work, showered, or changed out of your pajamas in three days, weeks, or even months to years at a time. Even something as simple as brushing your teeth can feel like an overwhelming task—one that you do not have the energy to face.

In addition to being diagnosed with MDD, they started treating me for Obsessive Compulsive Disorder (OCD). With Obsessive Compulsive Disorder, you have excessive thoughts (obsessions) that lead to repetitive behaviors (compulsions), such as picking, and low serotonin levels in the brain. Obsessive Compulsive Disorder is characterized by extreme perfectionism, accompanied by compulsive habits.

OCD has three main elements:
- **Obsessions**—unwanted, intrusive, and often distressing thoughts, images, or urges repeatedly enter your mind.
- **Emotions**—the obsession causes a feeling of intense anxiety or distress.
- **Compulsions**—are repetitive behaviors or mental acts. A person with OCD feels driven to perform as a result of the anxiety and distress caused by the obsession.

Obsessions may include:
- Doubts about not doing something right, such as turning off the stove or locking a door.
- Fears of saying or shouting inappropriate things in public.
- Unpleasant sexual images.

Compulsions may include:
- Hand washing due to fear of germs.
- Counting and recounting. A person cannot be sure they added it correctly.
- Check repeatedly to see if the curling iron is off.

OCD disrupts daily routines with intrusive thoughts and compulsive behaviors, often adding extra time to simple tasks and frustration when you cannot turn the obsessive thoughts off. On many occasions, it has intensified my anxiety, especially when I have had to turn the car back around to double-check, causing me to be late to my destination, including my workplace.

I was hospitalized for a couple of weeks—after discharge and sent back home with a medical treatment plan to continue to follow. What we thought was our worst nightmare had only just begun. I would continue to dig the grave of Sheol (the biblical meaning to the Hebrew mind: Sheol was simply the state or abode of the dead). Death was constantly pounding on my door—Goliath seemed to have the upper hand.

Empty Emily was written based on my lived experience with my mental health.

Empty Emily

She's been saved

Since the young age of 6

Amazing Grace played

Boy, she won't forget

She was little

But in her heart believed

She found God and

He was all she'd need

Out of the blue

Suddenly at 23

She was lost, sick

Her life had changed dramatically

Her faith was gone her
Reflection she could not see
The girl she once was
The girl she used to be

Empty Emily
Nothing left inside
Empty Emily
All she did was cry
Blinded by the love
He so freely gave that day
Emily
Lives far away

One would think
At the age of 25
This girl would be tired
Of riding that same old ride
No one knows how
Stubborn is she
The mask she wore to
Keep her dignity

No one knows this
World she lives alone
Emily seems to
Call this world her home

It is where she feels safe
So that's where she wants to stay
There she goes now
Running away

Empty Emily
Nothing left inside
Empty Emily
All she did was cry
Blinded by the love
He so freely gave that day
Empty Emily
Lives far away

It took so long to see
In the 2 years lost
All Emily had to do
Was look towards the cross

Empty Emily
Nothing left inside
Empty Emily
All she did was cry
Blinded by the love
He so freely gave that day
Empty Emily
Lives far away

Empty Emily

Run now Emily

She is empty

Emily[5]

---

5 Jesslyn McCutcheon. *Empty Emily*. TuneCore, 9 June 2018. YouTube, http://youtu.be/ g4cPh-39A8c?si=DfaEznyd_7zCltTi.

CHAPTER 2

THE IMPENDING STORM

"Consider it pure joy, my brothers and sisters, whenever you face trials of many kinds, because you know that the testing of your faith produces perseverance. Let perseverance finish its work so that you may be mature and complete, not lacking anything."
—James 1:2-4

After my discharge from the hospital, I made several promises to myself: I would follow my medical treatment plan, take my prescribed medication, attend outpatient therapy, and keep up with my appointments.

My family watched me day in and day out around the clock out of fear. The first six months after a hospitalization are especially critical to the suicide survivor. The risk of another attempt remains high for that entire first year. They took turns sleeping in the same room with me, beside my bed. Each family member, mom, dad, big brother, and younger brother, took different shifts watching, afraid, and never truly understanding. Days stretched into weeks, weeks stretched into months, and still no improvement.

You can spend so long in the darkness that you start to think that the darkness is day, consistently bracing for the storm that looms each day. When I started different medications, all I seemed to face were the horrific side effects. In addition to the antidepressant, they added a mood stabilizer. Soon after, I gained nearly 30 pounds, deepening my depression. Every new prescription came with a laundry list of side effects. My parents could not communicate with doctors; after all, I was over 18 and officially an adult. Self-care became a distant memory; my family had to force me to take a shower or clean up my room as if I were a child. If you knew me, you would not have recognized me. An unwelcoming look of hollowness and despair covered me, and I saw no value in myself. I felt like a filthy rag.

Severe depression is not something you can *snap out of, try harder,* or *keep to yourself*—this is a serious medical condition that demands attention. Even when you do receive help, there is an inner voice saying, *what if I am seen as my diagnosis and not as a person?* While brain scans are not used to diagnose bipolar disorder, they help researchers understand how the impact affects the brain and the body. Research has shown that those with bipolar disorder have decreased gray matter in their brain, which is detectable on a brain scan.

Mental illness does not have a particular look. However, when you are in deep depression, neglecting your hygiene, and avoiding self-care, it can manifest physically. On the other hand, when you are masking your depression, still trying to look like you do to others, no one would suspect a thing. I had mastered the art of faking it. I was the best actress, pretending everything was fine when I was barely hanging on–this type of darkness you do not want to enter. Depression is not just sadness; it is an absence of feeling—a numbness that makes you question your worth and your purpose. It is a thief wanting to take everything from you–your energy, hope, dreams, and willingness to fight. Depression can take over every aspect of your life, especially when it becomes so debilitating you can no longer function. Everything around you begins to wither away like flower petals.

At this point, I was unable to work. Getting out of bed felt like a monumental task. It is necessary to understand that while we may share similar experiences, each person experiencing depression has a unique journey. What works for one person may not work for the other. In this season, the depression lingered like an unwelcome visitor. You can develop this I do not care attitude because a part of you has already decided that you are incapable of facing this monster, this overwhelming giant. You can start to think that you do not stand a chance of surviving. Unable to see through the thick fog, you can only bump into brick walls. The amount of strength it takes to beat severe depression takes everything in you to make it through the day. To function, you need to adopt a warrior-like mentality. For the days you are unable to, that is okay. Small goals and steps.

I know that I have taken a couple of steps forward when I am wrestling with depression and can shower again. The days prior, it demanded everything in me to put two feet on the floor.

How is one supposed to beat disabling depression like this? The shadow of despair is unwilling to release its tight grip on you. I was always a well-groomed, self-disciplined, bright person with a bubbly personality. My very countenance changed as if controlled by some dark, evil inner spirit. Not only was I unkempt, I was mean to myself. Some of my behaviors became very strange and unusual. I made rash and impulsive decisions, not caring what it would do to me or my body. To get out of bed, I numbed the pain with alcohol, spending sprees, and smoking.

I did not have a sleeping schedule. I slept all day and would only come out of my room at night, if at all. I did the exact opposite of anything good. If I managed to go anywhere, I would take off in my car and drive, never having an end destination. Driving became a risk. I did not care how fast I was going. I had been pulled over a handful of times and received speeding tickets. Each time, I did not know where I was going, trying to escape the constant state of the tormenting hell that I was in. I would do anything to try and release the nagging intrusive thoughts and the emptiness inside my soul. I remember one day walking into my bathroom, standing in front of the mirror, opening the drawer, and grabbing the scissors, and without hesitation, I started to cut my hair. I had long hair that went down my back. I walked out of the bathroom with hardly any hair left on my head. My new haircut loudly affected the war going on inside.

All the horrible decisions I made were impulsive and harmful. I was out to destroy myself in any way possible. I still had a heartbeat, but I felt dead inside.

A journal from my mother:

Journal, July 14, 2000

Dear Lord,

I am at my lowest point in my life, Lord. My child is slowly slipping away, and my arm is not long enough to reach out and grab her. I can do nothing. My human instincts of love for her and my sense of protection and safeguarding for her are not enough. What do we do? Where do I turn? I know you are God Almighty, but you are so far away. When did I lose you? When did I lose my direction? I call and call upon your name, but you do not hear me. If you do, Lord, why are the answers so unsure? Why can't I see what you expect of me with Jesslyn and myself regarding her? It is so hard to say that my daughter tried to end her life and kill herself. What has caused her to reach this level of despair? Did we not teach a sound foundation in Christ? Did we not love enough or give enough? It seems our children are the victims of us as parents. Have we done such a horrific job? Help me.

Living with depression, at times, you feel as if you are fighting a battle you are never going to win, and you are fighting all alone. It is an isolating illness, making you feel like you are unable to connect or explain to others why you are struggling. The sense of shame that comes with this illness is not just emotional but paralyzing. It only compounds another layer to what you are already facing.

I tried for many years to fight this battle alone. Except you can not. If you can handle something this large by yourself, you will not be willing to listen to anyone. I understand the shame that comes with living with a mental illness—the kind of shame that makes you want to hide from the world. God has good things in store for those who trust in the healing power of Christ, which can set you free. God changes your identity when the devil wants to define you by your scars.

I realized that I could not navigate living with a mental illness solely through my wisdom. I recognized that I was not alone; I was a daughter of the King-I was seen. Whenever I took my eyes off Christ, I stumbled and failed—every time. Living with a mental illness requires time and takes patience.

During times of crisis, I found it crucial not to set aside the Word, as the cost of doing so is far too great. His Spirit will not respond until you engage your spirit and heed the teachings of the Word. For many years, I could not see that I was never forsaken, even in my darkest moments. However, this is furthest from what is true. Even in your deepest valley, He will continue to lead you. The night may seem victorious, but through Christ, you can prevail and overcome it. Remember, you are never too far gone for God to love you. Replace the deceptive thoughts with His Truth.

The grace of God has never been about fairness. It flows from the very nature of His character-loving, just, and kind. If you look at the world, you will see the beauty of nature created by His hands. His goodness shows up when we do not experience His direct interventions by placing others in our lives: my husband, children, mom, friends, family, brothers, and sisters in Christ.

When you reflect on the boundaries Jesus crossed in the Bible, it is truly inspiring! He did not care about societal labels or conditions. Jesus treated everyone equally. Do you think, even for a moment, that He loves us any less because we live with mental illness?

One of my favorite stories in the Gospels is when Jesus talks with the Samaritan woman at the well. For over 700 years, there was constant division between the Jews and the Samaritans. The Jews would go out of their way to not go through Samaria. Any Jewish traveler would walk around Samaria—not this Jesus. Jesus was tired and thirsty from His journey and sat by Jacob's well. At the same time, a Samaritan woman chose to go in the heat of the day and not earlier because the other women shunned her. How many times have you felt marginalized by people because you live with a mental illness? I know I have.

When she came to draw water, Jesus said, "Will you give me a drink?" (John 4:7). This surprised her because Jews typically avoided interaction with Samaritans due to their longstanding ethnic and religious tensions. Her face was cold and impassive. Jesus answered her, "If you knew the gift of God and who it is that asks you for a drink, you would have asked him and he would have given you living water." "Sir," the woman said, "you have nothing to draw with and the well is deep" (John 4:10-11). She wanted to know where she could get this living water. In their time and conversations with each other, Jesus revealed His deep knowledge of how she had five husbands and was currently living with a man who was not her husband. After Jesus said these words to her, she was amazed and thought Jesus was a prophet. Later in the conversation, Jesus explains to her that there will come a time when we will "worship in spirit and truth" (John 4:23-24). From their conversation, she believed that Jesus might be the Messiah. Leaving her water jar behind, she rushed back to her village to share what she had encountered.

Despite the Samaritan background or past mistakes, Jesus does not treat her differently. He treats her compassionately, prompting her to spread the good news to others. We should be treating others who live with a mental illness or any other disability—with compassion and the willingness to understand.

The Samaritan woman must have felt like she no longer belonged —carrying the weight of rejection and the hidden pain behind her eyes. But everything changed when she met the Savior face to face. Jesus had been waiting for her all along. He was waiting there for me, and He is waiting there for you. Jesus knows the pain of rejection and being misunderstood. The religious leaders of his time did not always agree with Him and His teachings, yet He remained faithful in His love and how He treated others. Your worth is not defined by whether you fit in; being a son or daughter of the highest King determines your value. Your paths will be washed with rivers of grace when you know Jesus.

A letter from my grandfather, Grandpaw Geras:

I only heard about your illness a little time ago from your dad. I'm sorry you have to endure the suffering of depression. I know what it is and do not want you to suffer from this insidious illness. Believe me, Jesslyn, I know more about your illness than you think. My wife suffered from the same illness. It took its toll on me because I had to care for her. The difference is now you have better medication and care. My experience with this illness is that you have to want to get better. Believe me, you can get better. Don't ever give up. It will take time. How long depends on you. I love you very much. You will make me happy again when you can get back to life.

I am praying for you. Remember, you must take a course of action that changes your thinking. I went through a bout with depression when I was in my forties. It is a chemical disorder that can be conquered, but you have to take care and do what is necessary to fight back. It is an insidious illness that creeps up on you slowly without you knowing it and takes hold. I think it is the devil's work. But the good news is you will get better. It is up to you how fast you will recover. Remember to try not to keep thinking about the illness. I love you and don't want you to suffer.

The same question rolled around over and over in my mind. How could a good, loving God allow this to happen? Pain has a way of twisting you up inside—leaving you feeling tangled and trapped. It can drive you to act in ways you never thought possible. Pain often brings an anger that feels like it will never stop pounding on the door of your heart. You begin to live in fear of the thoughts that plague your mind that never seem to let up, causing you to ask, *Where were you when I needed you the most?* You cannot see the truth because our eyes are not fully opened. We were never meant to carry this weight of pain by ourselves. Only God can give you a reason to keep going when you are trapped like this. There is no quick fix to take away this kind of deep pain. If you do not surrender to the feet of Jesus, you'll forget why and what you were created for.

The legacy of this kind of pain started with the brokenness of Adam and Eve disobeying God in the Garden of Eden. Since then, humanity has lived in a place of brokenness. Our world today sees the pain of Adam and Eve's sinful nature everywhere we turn. We have witnessed lives shattered and in desperate need of reconstruction. Because of the sting of pain of humanity's first sin, there is a separation between you and the Father because of the sting of pain.

However, hope is given to us in 1 Corinthians 15:45 when Paul writes, "So it is written: 'The first man Adam became a living being; the last Adam, a life-giving spirit. The spiritual did not come first, but the natural, and after that the spiritual.'" Jesus and the last Adam and the Son of God were sent for this reason. To save us from our sins and to free us from this pain, all this suffering.

It took me years to get through the deep-seated pain of accepting that I have a mental illness. It did not seem fair—life did not seem to make sense. I could not understand the *why* for years; maybe some of you reading this feel that exact way today. I had to come to terms with and internalize the truth of Isaiah 55:8-9, "For my thoughts are not your thoughts, neither are your ways my ways," declares the Lord. "As the heavens are higher than the earth, so are my ways higher than your ways and my thoughts than your thoughts." Our human thoughts are influenced by what we see now and are often driven by our emotions. We focus on the temporary—while His thoughts are eternal. Trusting in His ways and not our own brings peace. Praise God!

There are some questions we will never know the answers to. Why? Because we cannot see the whole picture. We are not God—we do not always know what is good and what is not. We cannot judge. We do not know what a day may bring, but we know God is good. I pushed God away many times in the pain. I did not understand. I felt like I was unable to reach Him, which led to frustration and withdrawal. I was not asking the right questions. We need to be asking questions.

Instead of only seeing the pain, we can ask ourselves, *What is God trying to teach me during this time? Am I still pursuing His purpose for my life while I wait? What might God be protecting me from or preparing me for?* Fast forward 25 years later, how breathtakingly beautiful what God has done in my life and continues to do through my ministry, Fighting Goliath for Mental Illness which helps empower women who live with bipolar disorder to manage their symptoms more effectively by providing resources, sharing our lived experiences, and incorporating His Word, allowing them to live more fulfilling lives. 1 Corinthians 13:12 conveys, "For now we see only a reflection as in a mirror; then we shall see face to face. Now I know in part; then I shall know fully, even, as I am fully known." Comfort is found in knowing we do not have to have all the answers and knowing that His ways are just.

I continued to fall short, I was weak. Whether I could still arise from the ashes time after time only changed when I finally let go, looked up, and never looked back down. I know that I cannot afford to take my eyes off Jesus. The only voice that can help me cut the silence when I fall into depression is the voice of God. We need to be deepening our faith through the pain. During these times, you have to lean in—HARD. You cannot leave prayer out of your life! My suffering led me to where I am with my ministry and my life today. There is a bigger purpose for all this pain, but you must allow time for your healing and reflection on what He is asking. Not what you want to do. You can deepen your relationship with God by surrendering in time of prayer, worship, and Scripture. Actual knowledge of God is what is within your heart and soul. Knowing God is not the same as studying theology. When you know God, nothing compares to feeling His presence. It is an emotion of incredible awe and joy.

We have to learn how to navigate through these storms when they arise in our lives. To navigate the never-ending storm of living with a chronic mental health condition. We have to stay the course and keep moving forward in faith. God does allow suffering to happen. But God also allows your suffering to be used for the good. As humans, we long for things to be made right. He knew that in our suffering, many would rebel against Him. But He also knew many would choose to follow Him. All pain has a purpose—even when you cannot see it. "And we know that in all things God works for the good of those who love him, who have been called according to his purpose" (Romans 8:28). As long as we live, we will experience suffering. When you believe and have a relationship with God, He makes these promises to those who love Him. My most intimate moments with God were in the dark. When you live to draw near to God, you see your pain through a different lens. I hope you embrace leaning in when your foot slips and you are out of options.

One day, maybe not today, you could say, thank you. *Thank You, Jesus, for the blood applied to my life*. When the pain feels overwhelming or too much to bear, take a moment to pause, breathe, and lean into prayer and Scripture. Give yourself grace, take it one step at a time, one day at a time, and practice self-care. Talking to someone you trust, practicing gratitude, and seeking connection with people who understand and support you is vital. Joining support groups can also be helpful. You are not alone. Above all, keep your eyes fixed on the Lord. No idea or opinion in this world will ever be more powerful than the Word of God and to let go to say, "Here I Am, Lord."

I started to write the lyrics to the song below, *Here I Am, Lord*, before I was hospitalized again for suicidal ideation. My mom found the lyrics unfinished and helped me complete writing the song while hospitalized.

Here I Am, Lord

In a world full of heartache, sin, and despair
Jesus cried, my child, I am here.
In fear and doubt, my ears could not hear
The voice of my Father saying, Come here.

So I looked to the Heavens with tears in my eyes
Through the dark and shadows, God heard me when I cried

Here I am, Lord
Standing in Your presence
Here I am, Lord
Calling out Your name
Here I am, Lord
Pleading for an answer
Here I am, Lord
Once again

Our lives are unpredictable,
with sudden changes everywhere
Who is the sense of strength
The one who always cares?
Jesus Christ, the majestic One
The past, the present is He
Jesus Christ, the majestic One
I'll tell you, He's the key

So I look to the Heavens with love in my eyes
With Christ in my heart, God heard me when I cried

Here I am, Lord
Standing in Your presence
Here I am, Lord
Calling out Your name

Here I am, Lord
Pleading for an answer
Here I am, Lord
Once again

You must never fear Him
He will show you the way
He's the One and Only
I choose to serve this day

Here You are, Lord
Standing in my presence
Here You are, Lord, Calling out my name
Here You are, Lord, Giving me an answer
Here You are, Lord
Always the same
Always the same[6]

---

6   McCutcheon, Jesslyn., and Geras, Cheryl. *Here I Am, Lord, 2013*

CHAPTER 3

THIS MEANS WAR

"Be strong in the Lord and in his mighty power. Put on the full armor of God, so that you can take a stand against the devil's schemes."
—Ephesians 6:10

I was my own worst enemy, trapped in a cycle of near-death experiences that left scars on my soul–my past haunted me, relentless and unforgiving. I felt like I was constantly drowning, screaming for help as the waves pulled me under, gasping for air. I was never fully submerged; somehow, I managed to surface enough to see another day.

How many chances does one person get? My reserves of grace and mercy had long run dry, yet He remained a gracious and merciful God, offering an unconditional love I had not earned. I needed to understand that He does not keep track of how many chances He gives. It is not about how often we fall short but about the unwavering constancy of the love of the Father for you and me.

My faith wavered, shifting like the many colors of my emotions. I knew I was a daughter of the King, but I was stubborn and defiant—I was not listening or seeking restoration; I was sabotaging myself. My illness was all I could see. Scripture calls us to recondition ourselves, to renew our minds daily. "Do not conform to the pattern of this world, but be transformed by the renewing of your mind. Then you will be able to test and approve what God's will is—his good, pleasing and perfect will" (Romans 12:2). Yet every time I seemed to get back on my feet, I was knocked down again, with Satan's mocking, his hysterical laughing in my ears. As Louie Giglio warns, "Don't give the enemy a seat at your table."[7] It is time to put a smooth stone in your slingshot and experience unwavering faith that God is Mightier and Bigger, and His power will see you through.

Every medication change felt like starting over as my body struggled to cope with intolerable side effects. The search for the correct medication was exhausting and grueling—what worked for me would not necessarily work for someone else. Finding the right combination, or cocktail, took nearly a decade. Along the way, some medications we tried even exacerbated my symptoms. I spent many nights on the cold bathroom floor, so sick from nausea and vomiting.

The medications often felt more overpowering than the illness itself. I faced nearly debilitating side effects: extreme weight gain, hair loss, blurred vision, severe tremors (especially in my hands), unsteadiness in my balance, vomiting, diarrhea, sleepiness, dizziness, dry mouth, constipation, fainting, eye twitching, and uncontrollable muscle spasms. I learned these spasms were a condition called TD or Tardive Dyskinesia, which forces repeated movements. In a later chapter, I discuss being diagnosed with serotonin syndrome, a life-threatening reaction caused by an overload of serotonin my body could not process. Finding the correct medication can be challenging and, many times, a painful journey. Many people, understandably, forgo treatment altogether because of these side effects, hesitant to continue with any medication plan.

It is difficult to see clearly when your face is down in the dirt. Especially when you do not understand what is wrong with you or why you are not getting better, a crisis can arise if you do not understand, causing you not to take care of yourself as needed. It is crucial to address mental health before it escalates to a crisis level, recognizing the signs and symptoms early on instead of waiting until it is too late. I was often terrible at being an advocate for myself. There were many times when my doctor prescribed a mood stabilizer, and after

---

7   Giglio, Louie. *Don't Give the Enemy a Seat at Your Table: It's Time to Win the Battle of Your Mind.* Thomas Nelson, 2021.

starting to feel better, I mistakenly believed I no longer needed the medication. Without my doctor's consent, I would take myself off the medication, a move that is not only unwise but can also be hazardous if the drug is not tapered off correctly.

During my time serving on the National Alliance on Mental Illness (NAMI) Helpline, I learned about a term called anosognosia. This neurological condition makes individuals unaware of their own psychiatric or neurological deficits, and it is often associated with mental illness, dementia, and stroke. For example, you might stop taking your medication after getting back on your feet, thinking you no longer need to take what your doctor prescribed. The Henry Amador Center on Anosognosia is a non-profit organization that provides families and professionals with the tools to support individuals with mental illness.[8]

I lived for years without realizing I had a mental illness. My brain could not seem to perceive my symptoms accurately. I could not think enough to understand. According to NAMI, brain imaging studies have shown that this crucial area of the brain can be damaged by schizophrenia and bipolar disorder as well as by diseases like dementia. When the frontal lobe is not operating at 100%, a person may lose—or partially lose—the ability to update one's self-image.

Living with a mental illness can often feel like a battle on multiple fronts. Many individuals describe this feeling as being attacked by something larger than themselves, sometimes attributing it to a spiritual conflict against Satan and his weapons of mass destruction. He specializes in anger, suffering, pain, grief, and loss. It is hard for anyone to see a way forward during these times.

I lived in overwhelming darkness, feeling isolated and doubtful that anyone would understand my pain. My inner voice screamed worthlessness, convincing me that I would never achieve the victory of recovery. For those of us who view our lives through a spiritual lens, it often feels like a tormenting battle against endless negative

---

8 "The Henry Amador Center on Anosognosia." *Leap Institute*, www.leapinstitute.org.

thoughts. I would disengage, unable to find the strength to fight back, and my anger grew into bitterness, taking control of my actions and preventing me from moving past anything.

The cycle felt never-ending, marked by medication changes, hospitalizations, doctor appointments, ECT treatments, and their accompanying side effects. I was stuck in a hamster wheel, constantly spinning but never progressing. At times, I felt like a mental health experiment, wondering what medication would be next on the list. I hated myself and what was happening to my life.

I knew I needed to address the anger from feeling like a health experiment because if I did not, things would begin to spiral out of control. The only way to overcome the bitterness of living with a serious mental illness—or any life-altering event—is through God, finding contentment in His presence. I was relieved to find out after the official diagnosis of bipolar I—much of the anger stemmed from living with bipolar disorder. Here are some key differences:

THE DIFFERENCE BETWEEN ANGER AND BIPOLAR ANGER

Problem	Anger	Bipolar Anger
Trigger	External event or situation	May have no clear trigger
Proportionality	Generally proportional	Often disproportionate
Accompanying Symptoms	None typically	Linked to mood disorder
Duration	Short-lived	May last longer or shift quickly

If bipolar anger is affecting you or someone you know, it is essential to recognize it as part of the disorder and seek appropriate medical support.

Spiritually, neglecting to confront anger can lead to poison that threatens one's spirit. Ephesians 4:31-32 reminds us, "Get rid of all bitterness, rage and anger, brawling and slander, along with every form of malice. Be kind and compassionate to one another, forgiving each other, just as in Christ God forgave you." For individuals struggling with mental illness, these feelings can often exacerbate symptoms. By consciously working to release these emotions, we can create space for healing and healthier mental states. Reflecting on Ephesians 4:31-32 can encourage us to focus on healing from our internal struggles and external relationships. It serves as an essential reminder of emotional health, forgiveness, and compassion, all of which play significant roles in our journey. In doing so, we can cultivate a positive mindset that can be a part of our healing process.

At this point in my life, I struggled to see the purpose because of my suffering. I questioned how anything good could emerge from it and wrestled with what God was trying to achieve through my pain. My anger isolated me, driving away friends, costing me jobs, straining family relationships, and creating a chasm between me and God. I felt utterly disconnected from everything I once valued, consumed by turmoil. It felt like my life had come to a complete standstill—as if it were already over.

As humans, we do not see suffering as a positive thing. It is hard to see through the fog in these moments that anything good can come from all of this. I went from valley to valley. He does not take joy in seeing us in agony, but sometimes, a crisis is needed to lead you back into His loving arms. Sometimes, you have to visit hell to get back to heaven. Sometimes, your heart has to break to find your soul again. We can be committed to God, go to church, dress the part, and be kind people, but if our souls have not fully surrendered, we will keep running in circles.

I knew Jesus, but I convinced myself that I was never going to cross over the line into recovery to live a fulfilling life. After years of madness, achieving victory seemed to have been left behind. How can you tell if you have fully surrendered? You find the peace that only your Heavenly Father can provide. Even when the storms of life come my way now, I know that I am not alone in my struggles and that a higher power guides each step I take. I had to let go completely. Releasing the control, I had to learn to trust the process entirely, not partially.

It is challenging to embrace the unknowns of your future, but be confident that you will be okay no matter what, that is what faith is all about. I had to let go of a lot of emotional baggage that I had been carrying around with me that continued to weigh me down. I had to forgive myself for my past mistakes and failures. Your journey—both mentally and spiritually—is ongoing. It requires continual reflection, trust, and transformation with yourself, others, and God.

I cannot fight this battle without a firm foundation of Jesus Christ. He is the rock on which I stand—greatest treasure of my longing soul. Without Him, I wandered in the desert like the Israelites did for 40 years, trying to get to the Promised Land. They wandered because they needed stronger faith. I needed to learn, just like the Israelites. I needed to decrease, and He needed to increase for me to fight. I needed to grow my spiritual development within myself, and I needed to find my identity in Christ.

Being faithful often involves experiencing failure. Over the years, I have had to learn how to survive by choosing whether to rely on God or continue trying to handle everything independently. That philosophy never got me very far. Without grounding ourselves in prayer, we will forever be spinning our wheels. We must never stop praying; it provides the strength and courage to stand firm in our faith. Pray for a hedge of protection around yourself and your family against spiritual attacks. Pray for wisdom and discernment. Pray for forgiveness and healing, for community support, and the renewing of your mind, and for ultimate victory in Christ. The apostle Paul addressed this in the book of Romans:

Or don't you know that all of us who were baptized into Christ Jesus were baptized into his death? We were therefore buried with him through baptism into death in order that, just as Christ was raised from the dead through the glory of the Father, we too may live a new life. For if we have been united with him in a death like his, we will certainly also be united with him in a resurrection like his. For we know that our old self was crucified with him so that the body ruled by sin might be done away with, that we should no longer be slaves to sin—because anyone who has died has been set free from sin (Romans 6:3-7).

Humans can stray from our paths and lose their way, often being thrown off track by the circumstances For many years, my relationship with sin and the choices I made during my battle with my mental health were misguided. I often inflicted hardship on myself due to my state of mind and the failure to trust Christ as I needed to. I was caught in a constant spiritual battle, doubting whether I would ever recover and achieve what everyone who lives with bipolar disorder desires—a fulfilling life. Worry and fear consumed me, leaving me tense, uncomfortable, and threatened.

My fear was unhealthy and certainly not from God. The apostle Paul reminds us in 2 Timothy 1:7, "For the Spirit God gave us does not make us timid, but gives us power, love and self-discipline." God does not instill fear that cripples us with anxiety or paralyzes us. While anxiety can be a fear of living with bipolar disorder, it is not from God. Instead, His divine power equips us with strength, courage, and love to face our challenges confidently. At the time, I lacked self-discipline and did not give myself a chance to try and survive. Though I recognized the importance of managing my mental health, I neglected my spiritual well-being, allowing fear to overshadow what mustard seed of faith I had left.

What if all you truly need is Jesus? I wrestled constantly with the overwhelming thoughts of whether I could even live with this illness. It felt too big—impossible to manage. I could not see beyond the suffering, the pain. Although I was not consciously following a dark path, the battles in my mind continued to rage, and I could not find any trace of light.

Sometimes, the pit or black hole would swallow me for days, weeks, months, or even years. Daily, I was not wearing the whole armor of God, nor did I fully understand how to care for myself living with bipolar disorder. I was not pursuing His wisdom or walking wisely. To walk wisely, you need determination, focus, trust, courage, perseverance, and the Holy Spirit.

Instead, I believed many lies. I doubted I would ever get married, have a family, or know the joy of motherhood. Would I even be a good mom? How could I care for a child when I struggled to care for myself? I felt far behind my friends—many were already married and starting families. I, on the other hand, was in and out of hospitals, fighting to stay alive.

The name *devil* means *slanderer*. He wants our souls so Christ cannot claim them. The enemy's nature is void of truth and light. He is the father of lies, a *liar* by definition. John 8:44 says, "You belong to your father, the devil, and you want to carry out your father's desires. He was a murderer from the beginning, not holding to the truth, for there is no truth in him. When he lies, he speaks his native language, for he is a liar and the father of lies." One cannot put on just one single piece and expect to be shielded. The darts will keep finding their mark unless we are equipped with the proper protection for the fight.

In Ephesians 6:10-18, the Apostle Paul used this imagery to encourage believers to rely on His strength and protection. Each piece is created to stand firm against our life temptations, challenges, and spiritual battles.

- **The Belt of Truth:**

    Paul speaks about the belt of truth in Ephesians 6:13, "Therefore put on the full armor of God, so that when the day of evil comes, you may be able to stand your ground, and after you have done everything, to stand." The belt was a part of the Roman attire. It helps us hold off the enemy and stand on our feet in truth. The truth of His Word. As David said in Psalm 119:11, "I have hidden your word in my heart that I might not sin against you." Everything else will fall into place when we live in His Truth. "If you hold to my teaching, you are my disciples. Then you will know the truth, and the truth will set you free" (John 8:31-32).

- **The Breastplate of Righteousness:**

  The breastplate was to guard the heart. One strike from the enemy could mean life or death. We are to live in righteousness— to live justly. Righteousness is living by His biblical standards. Your heart is the main vital organ that God wants from you. You are unique. Your soul makes up your mind, emotions, will, and your conscience. All three work together through prayer, reading scripture, and self-reflection. Our minds and emotions will work in harmony with one another. Your mind is the devil's target. He will fight to take you down; he will weaken your thought processes, and steer you to destructive temporary behavior like excessive eating, not eating at all, driving too fast, and drinking alcohol in excess. The list could go on. He could turn the table of your emotions into anger or revenge, taking you completely away from His Truth and His biblical guidelines. We have to guard, protect, and shield our hearts from the enemy who actively seeks to destroy us day after day.

- **The Shoes of Peace:**

  The devil would instead like to weigh you down with worry, anxiety, chaos, war, and strife–complete instability. He loves destroying the stillness of your mind, heart, body, and your relationships. He can make you doubt what kind of parent you are, what your talents and gifts are, that your dreams are out of reach. If we learn to trust in the Lord, He will keep us in perfect harmony, not a chaotic state of mind. In the Old Testament, the Hebrew word for peace is *shalom*. Shalom refers to a place of complete wholeness. The Greek word found in the New Testament for shalom is *Eirene*, which expanded on the meaning. Eirene closely mirrors shalom and describes a holistic state of well-being that extends into spiritual, relational, and communal harmony. Life is complex and full of moving parts. Life constantly needs to be restored. To complete or make restoration. To recognize and heal broken relationships, you bring shalom. Solomon tells us in Proverbs 16:7, "When the Lord takes pleasure in anyone's way, he causes their enemies to make peace with them." Jesus told us, "Peace I leave with you; my peace I give you. I do not give to you as the world gives. Do not let your hearts be troubled and do not be afraid" (John 14:27). True *shalom* is restoring wholeness to the brokenness in our lives. True peace comes from knowing God.

- **The Shield of Faith:**

"Every word of God is flawless; he is a shield to those who take refuge in him" (Proverbs 30:5). Ancient historians say these shields were so big that when a soldier was crouched down, the shield could cover the whole body. Talking about faith is not the same thing as having faith. "As the body without the spirit is dead, so faith without deeds is dead" (James 2:26). Having faith is having a lifestyle by what God calls you to do. You choose to have faith even when you cannot see the outcome–even when all you seem to encounter is storm after storm. The shield of faith is our protection from the enemy. "In addition to all this, take up the shield of faith with which you can extinguish all the flaming arrows of the evil one" (Ephesians 6:16).

- **The Helmet of Salvation:**

It is time to win the battle of your mind! The process of sanctification is one that we are constantly working on renewing our minds by putting on the helmet of salvation. When you are not applying salvation to your life, you are still vulnerable to being under attack. You will face many trials and tribulations, even if saved, but you can find comfort in knowing He is standing in the battle. "But since we belong to the day, let us be sober, putting on faith and love as a breastplate, and the hope of salvation as a helmet" (1 Thessalonians 5:8). For my friends who live with a brain-based illness—the helmet's primary function for the soldier was to protect his skull and brain in battle. When we choose to set the helmet aside, our minds are no longer protected and exposed to the swift swings of the enemy. Wear a helmet! Know that you are worthy, loved, capable, forgivable, known, and not a mistake. We have already been paid in full by our Savior. "For it is by grace you have been saved, through faith—and this is not from yourselves, it is the gift of God" (Ephesians 2:8).

- **The Sword of the Spirit:**

  The sword of the Spirit is the weapon of the Word of God. How do we fight? We do not just believe; we take action. You read your Bible daily. You study the Word. You believe and proclaim the truth of God. You evaluate yourself in the light of what His Word says. The purpose of the sword of the Spirit is defense. For the Word of God is alive and active. Sharper than any double-edged sword, it penetrates even to divide soul and spirit, joints and marrow; it judges the thoughts and attitudes of the heart. Nothing in all creation is hidden from God's sight. Everything is uncovered and laid bare before the eyes of him to whom we must give account" (Hebrews 4:12-13).

Why is it so hard to pray at times when you and depression are face-to-face? Depression can create a sense of isolation and disconnection from others, including from God. Many times, depression saps motivation and energy, making the most minor tasks feel overwhelming. The thought of praying may lack the mental or emotional strength to engage. The hopelessness one feels while in depression can make a person feel trapped. The spiritual warfare in your head tells you it is not worth the effort this time.

When I find myself at a loss for words and struggling to think clearly, I repeat a short yet powerful verse: "I lift up my eyes to the mountains—where does my help come from? My help comes from the LORD, the maker of heaven and earth" (Psalm 121:1-2). I say it over and over until it resonates within me. You must believe what you are saying. You cannot just say the words. You must believe it!

Ask yourself this question: *How often have you attempted to do something without making God your cornerstone? How far did it get you?* I would dare to go out on a limb and say not that far. Time and again, I have learned that I cannot succeed without Christ as the foundation in every thought, decision, and action I take. You might manage to get by for some time, but eventually, your broken heart will continue to ache. The only One who will ever love you unconditionally is Jesus. His love is sacrificial, demonstrated through His willingness to lay down His life on the cross. The ultimate sacrifice reveals the depth of His love, and He took on suffering, shame, and death to restore our broken relationship with God.

Family may let you down, friends might even walk away, and you might only have a dollar left to your name. We are not promised a life without trials, but we are promised that God will be with us every step of the way. "The Lord gave and the Lord has taken away; may the name of the Lord be praised" (Job 1:21). We must trust in God, even in the face of adversity, because everything happens for a purpose.

Job was a godly man. He loved God. As the events in his life started to unravel, Satan was sure Job would turn on God. He lost his oxen, donkeys, sheep, servants, and camels. Cutting even deeper came his sons and daughters. "Naked I came from my mother's womb, and naked I will depart. The Lord gave and the Lord has taken away; may the name of the Lord be praised" (Job 1:21). When that did not turn Job from His presence, the infliction continued by taking his health. Job had his faith and still endured this level of suffering. The point is that we are not to question His sovereignty. He owes us no explanation. Even when your world is falling around you, He expects us to trust Him. Eventually, all the losses that Job bore were restored twofold. We must trust that He is in control, and we are not by putting on the whole armor of God.

The greatness of God far surpasses anything we can comprehend. There is no one like Him. He desires not just a part of you but all of you. In my struggle, paranoia and anxiety tormented my mind, leaving me with no peace. The fear I carried loomed over me like a haunting nightmare. I would cry out in anguish, scream in frustration, and clench my fists in anger as tears streamed down my face, grappling with the overwhelming *why* of it all. In moments of despair, I raged against my pain, hurting myself, breaking things in my path, and slamming doors. There were times I even cursed the day I was born.

Your brain is a complex organ. Your brain controls thought, memory, emotion, vision, breathing, touch, the beating of your heart, and the digestion of your food. Your brain is the center core for controlling all your body functions.

In the beginning, my family and I endured three grueling years that we often referred to as hell. It took that long to find any correct treatments for my diagnosis. Numerous times people can and will be diagnosed with multiple diagnoses over time. Living with bipolar disorder can feel like being trapped on a relentless roller coaster, where every day is a fight to stay alive and to be able to function in society. I never knew when the depression or mania might seize me again, leaving me drained of the strength or will to keep going. Bipolar disorder can feel like a vicious cycle, threatening to consume you unless you acknowledge its seriousness. If you are not careful, the misery can linger until you accept that managing this illness is a lifelong journey that will take courage to live with. Ultimately, the responsibility for your choices lies within you. The harsh truth is that no one else can fix you, no matter how hard they want to. But through it all, God is there, offering strength, reminding us we are not alone, and sustaining us through every trial.

My life was agony and misery for many years trying to navigate finding my way. Besides my first suicide attempt in the beginning stages, I have faced suicidal ideation at various points throughout my journey whenever the weight of my burdens became too much to bear. I asked, just like the prophet Elijah hiding in the wilderness from the wicked Queen Jezebel, for God to please take my life. Elijah had just experienced a powerful demonstration of His power when he called down fire from heaven to consume his offering, proving the Lord's power over Baal (1 Kings 18:20-39). Following this, Elijah commanded and executed the false prophets; additionally, Queen Jezebel threatened his life in retaliation for his actions. He became fearful and ran for his life.

At night, I would pray for God to take me while I slept, to rescue me from this misery and silence the tormenting thoughts. To turn the thoughts off. Like Elijah, I was terrified; it was more than a struggle to see another way out—pure agony. *Would the bondage ever end? Would the chains ever break?* As John 10:10 reminds us, "The thief comes only to steal, and kill, and destroy; I have come that they may have life and have it to the full." Satan is hell-bent on poisoning us with the goodness of God, ready to choke the very breath out of us if we allow it. The fight felt never-ending like thunder rolling in with waves crashing onto the shore. Satan's hateful darts pierced me one after another. Who was I to think that I could handle this on my own? My human frame was not meant to bear this weight, this beast of an illness, all alone. Who was I to question the wisdom of God, our Creator? I am not the One capable of carrying others on the wings of an eagle. His vastness is a measure none of us can withstand. As Romans 16:20 promises, He will crush Satan under your feet. My story and testimony reveal that despite living with a mental illness, it is possible to have a fulfilling life when equipped with the right tools for both mental and spiritual health. By the end of this book, you will discover a victory I continue to win because I am fighting alongside the armies of the living God—He is no stranger to the scar.

I had to learn to leave behind all the burdens, the doubt, the feelings of worthlessness, and all the time spent in bed. The many times I have lost because I could not get out of bed. I had to forgive myself for being so behind the eight-ball. Life was not a race. I had to stop comparing myself to others and move at my own pace for my journey. I had to let go of all negative thinking—you will never be good enough, you are not talented enough, you have scars that make you feel ugly. Your battle wounds, my friends, mold you to being the one-of-a-kind person you are. Not a single scar will be wasted in the eyes of the Father.

I had to learn to be vulnerable and ask for help. I had to know that it was okay that I was not OK all the time. I had to learn self-love. To not only fill my mind with the Word of God but to continue to educate myself about mental illness and living with bipolar disorder. Little by little, I had to let people into this part of my life. I had to be vulnerable, which takes a tremendous amount of courage.

It can be challenging to find the right people to trust. The best way to find your people is to see who is there for you and who walks away from you when you need someone the most. Your people are the ones who did not leave you when you were at your worst. Your people are the ones who bring you the torch in the middle of the night. Your people are praying people. When you cannot find the words to pray for yourself, God can provide a circle of people to pray around you.

You can achieve freedom through the love of others. Do not continue to be in rooms where you do not feel welcomed or rooms where people refuse to understand you or the seriousness of the medical condition you live in. Be in rooms where you know when you are not there, people are still sticking up for you and who you are. Let God shut those doors that are not right for you and move on to the people who will love you for who you are. You are never alone.

When I finally learned to refocus my mindset on God and not focus on my illness or myself, I saw the stones rolling away one by one. How? By putting on the armor of God. I start my day in His Word by praying for the day ahead. Instead of complaining, I ask Him:

- To teach me to learn what I am supposed to do in that season. Embrace being honest with yourself and where you currently are.
- Put on the belt of truth.
- Seek to reflect His character by putting on the breastplate of righteousness and making choices that honor God. Not yourself.
- Wear the shoes of the gospel of peace by replacing the madness and your unquiet mind with the eternal Truth that never changes.
- Shield your life with the shield of faith by trusting God even in your lowest valley. The God of angel armies is on your side.
- Put on the helmet of salvation by reminding yourself that you are a child of God. Your identity is in Christ, not what the world offers.
- Memorize Scripture to equip yourself with the sword of His Word to help combat your negative thoughts, doubts, and fears.

Reflect on how you applied the armor of God to your life that day and consider what worked well and where you need to make changes. By incorporating a practical daily routine with the armor of God, you can start to watch your giants fall one by one. King David is credited traditionally for writing the below Psalm:

> You have searched me, Lord, and you know me.
> You know when I sit and when I rise; you perceive my thoughts from afar.
> You discern my going out of my lying down, you are familiar with all my ways.
> Before a word is on my tongue
> You Lord, know it completely.
> You hem me in behind and before, and you lay your hand upon me.
> Such knowledge is too wonderful for me,
> Too lofty for me to attain.

Where can I go from your Spirit?
Where can I flee from your presence?
If I go up the heavens, you are there;
If I make my bed in the depths, you are there.
If I rise on the wings of the dawn,
If I settle on the far side of the sea,
Even there your hand will guide me, your right hand will
hold me fast.
If I say, "Surely the darkness will hide me and the light be-
come night around me,"
Even the darkness will not be dark to you;
The night will shine like the day,
For darkness is as light to you.
For you created my inmost being;
You knit me together in my mother's womb.
I praise you because I am fearfully and wonderfully made;
Your works are wonderful,
I know that fully well.
My frame was not hidden from you
When I was made in the secret place,
When I was woven together in the depths of the earth.
Your eyes saw my unformed body;
All the days ordained for me were written in your book
Before one of them came to be (Psalm 139:1-16).

CHAPTER 4

GOING ROGUE

"They asked him, "Tell us, who is responsible for making all this trouble for us? What kind of work do you do? Where do you come from? What is your country? From what people are you?" He answered, "I am a Hebrew and I worship the Lord, the God of heaven, who made the sea and the dry land."
—Jonah 1:8-9

Completely broken and lost, I vanished repeatedly, desperate to escape. I had become an expert at resisting His plan, trapped in endless circles of rebellion that only deepened my pain. My mind was a whirlwind, thoughts spinning so rapidly that I would have done anything to make the thoughts stop. They jumped from one idea to the next, leaving my brain in overdrive. I took long, aimless drives, never knowing where I was going, with no plan or destination. Sometimes, I would be gone for days, indifferent to who might worry about me or whether anyone knew where I was. I caused my parents to worry sick over days of silence, unaware of the torment I was putting them through. At one point, they even issued an APB—an all-point bulletin—broadcasting an alert across police stations throughout the state because I had disappeared without a trace, leaving no word behind.

I was not thinking clearly. I was always on the run, though I had no idea what I was running toward or fleeing from—only that it was not God. My heart hardened under the weight of pain, convinced that nothing would ever change. After two years of mostly being homebound, living through endless highs and lows, it became nearly impossible to see any good in life. My family tiptoed around, walking on eggshells, always unsure of what I might do next. I refused to accept the reality of what I was going through. I would start my medication, only to stop again when the side effects grew unbearable or whenever I felt I could manage without it.

The illness was a constant, indescribable horror. It haunted me daily, and I could never seem to outrun it. I could not envision the purpose for my life. The road I was on was much too painful and daunting. My constant running only added to the dangerous storm I was already facing. Like the prophet Jonah, I sought to seek escape through isolation and avoidance rather than trusting God and the journey He had laid out for my life.

"Go to the great city of Nineveh and preach against it, because its wickedness has come up before me." (Jonah 1:2). God wanted Jonah to go and preach a message of repentance to the Assyrians for their corrupt behavior. Instead of heading toward Assyria, Jonah went rogue, going in the opposite direction, and boarded a ship bound for Tarshish. The Lord sent a great wind on the sea and caused the sailors to be afraid. He told the sailors that he was running from the Lord and worshiped the God of heaven, who made the sea and the dry land. Jonah plunged into the depths of the sea because of his running and disobedience. "'Pick me up and throw me into the sea,' he replied, 'and it will become calm. I know that it is my fault that this great storm has come upon you.' Then they took Jonah and threw him overboard, and the raging sea grew calm" (Jonah 1:12, 15).

God wants us to cry out to Him when we are in trouble. Instead of running and hiding, we must turn to Jesus, our Rock, the Light of the World. We will never be able to escape from His omniscience and omnipresence. He comforts the hurting, provides for our needs, strengthens us as believers, and forgives us when we repent. You have to turn to the truth when the lies take over—this can often be when we hit rock bottom. Moments when we realize we can no longer keep running. We have to be open to His intervention—this is when the surrender flag gets raised. We finally ask God for help or the guidance needed. You will never find the purpose of His plan for your life if you refuse to listen.

Through all the depression and the impulsive, erratic decisions, I was blind—too stubborn to see a way out. I was pulling a Jonah, running from the chance of recovery, unable to believe the storm in my life could ever be calm. Would my peace ever be still again? I could not see that I would ever recover from this raging storm. I did not focus my eyes on Christ, and I continued to sink, gasping for air. I could not find a balance between the cycles of my moods; each one felt like it had complete control. Depression would conquer me, pulling me into despair, while my impulsive decisions added to the chaos.

In those early years, I stayed hidden, like Jonah in the belly of the fish—not for three days and nights, but for weeks, months, even years. I wanted nothing to do with this life. The only way to quiet the noise of my mind was through sleep. I was terrified of living, gripped by fear for my safety, which kept me confined, unwilling to step into unknown territory. I was often irritable, and if my parents pushed me too far, I would respond with sudden, explosive outbursts. I would find my anger becoming more manifested when I was in a manic phase because of my impaired judgment and reduced impulse control. I was hypersensitive to people or situations that might seem minor to others. Some examples of hypersensitivity can be:

- **Sensitivity to criticism or rejection:**

  Someone with bipolar disorder might over analyze interactions, feeling hurt or misunderstood by a friend's casual remark or constructive feedback at work, which can lead to intense sadness, anger, or self-doubt.

- **Emotional reactions to minor situations:**

  Loud noises (someone chewing their food too loudly or making slurping noises), crowded places (concerts, large shopping centers), and bright lights can heighten sensory sensitivity to make it challenging to concentrate, navigate everyday living, or enjoy social events.

- **Disruption in your routine:**

  Sudden plans or daily routine changes can feel destabilizing, leading to frustration or distress. This unexpected turn of events can lead to anxiety or irritability.

- **Reliving your past mistakes or experiences:**

  People who live with bipolar disorder may experience memories of past failures, hurtful events or comments, and mistakes made. Often leading to a cascade of negative emotions, too.

Some people with bipolar disorder often feel isolated or misunderstood by those around them. Mild criticism or perceived rejection can feel deeply personal and lead to intense sadness, anger, or self-doubt. Someone with bipolar disorder might over analyze interactions, feeling hurt by casual constructive feedback at work.

As a child, I would never have dared talk back to my parents, show them disrespect, use curse words, or take the Lord's name in vain—such behavior would not be tolerated in our household. If a show on TV used His name carelessly, we were taught to change the channel. My parents raised us with a firm foundation, with Christ as our Cornerstone.

As the months stretched on, my mom could not bear to walk past my room every day and see me sleeping my life away, as if my life had come to a halt. She just wanted me to move, do something, do anything!

Whenever she urged me to get up, shower, or even open the blinds in my room, it grated on my last nerve. Her persistence stirred up annoyance and crossness in me; the more she pushed, the angrier I became. All I could see was red. She would pull back the curtains and let light in, and I would immediately follow right behind her, closing them back and pleading for her to leave me alone, and not in a loving way. The more she pushed, the more I would explode, saying things I could never take back, words that still haunt me. I was harsh and mean, and it felt like I was playing a dangerous game of dancing with the enemy. A game I was not winning.

I refused the light; I craved the darkness. I did not want any rays of sunlight seeping through the windows or peeking through the blinds. The darker the room, the better. I wanted to be in isolation and have nothing to do with the outside world. I only felt the grappling of confusion in my mind from the unknown of what I had become. I felt like there was no fight left in me. Who was this? What monster had I become?

My mother desperately wanted to help me, as did my entire family. However, you cannot fix someone living with bipolar disorder. The best thing you can do is walk alongside them, offering support, but again, the responsibility for healing lies solely with the person struggling in agony and misery. Each individual has a choice. Fight for their wellness, or give into the giant. You can do this! I am living proof you can do this!

I failed to recognize that I was being tested amidst all these trials, and one day, God would use my heartache to strengthen me. I was far from understanding that God had not forgotten me—far from grasping the truth of His promise: "Never will I leave you; never will I forsake you" (Hebrews 13:5). The only music I heard was bone-chilling silence.

The following journal entry was written by my mother on January 6, 2002, during a time when all hope seemed lost. My family lived each day uncertain of what it would bring, praying fervently that perhaps today, we would catch a glimpse of light amidst the darkness.

Journal, January 6, 2002

I will bless thee, oh Lord, with a heart of Thanksgiving. I will bless thee, oh Lord. Oh, Jesus, I am broken, as are my heart, soul, and very being. I ache for my daughter, yet she does not see or care. I cannot reach her. I know, Lord, you can give her life again. You represent to us a new life. Your forgiving power superseded any-thing we mortal humans could comprehend. Why can't we just be a happy family? Why can't we just connect? Should I always be looking for answers? I cannot ignore this problem: it exists. I cannot just walk away and never do anything. I look to you for my answers. Faith and belief that with God, all things are possible, yet the hopelessness for my daughter does not go away. Lord, I truly believe my daughter will be used for you through her mistakes and all. I believe you have a message to give to others through her—a message of forgiveness and strength. I have prayed for many years for you to use her. I give her to you! Now I understand that if I give her to Almighty God, you will deal with the problem. Not me. That is why you told me to be still. Thank you for your answer.

It seemed like we were out of options. None of the medications were lifting me from the severe, catatonic depression I was experiencing, and I was barely eating or drinking. As a last resort, I began a series of electroconvulsive therapy (ECT) treatments. According to the American Psychiatric Association, ECT is a medical procedure most often used for severe cases of major depression or bipolar disorder that have not responded to other treatments.[9] ECT involves brief electrical stimulation of the brain while the patient is under anesthesia, and it is administered by a trained team, including a psychiatrist, anesthesiologist, and nurse or physician assistant. During the procedure, small electric currents are passed through the brain, intentionally triggering a brief seizure. This process seems to alter brain chemistry in ways that can rapidly relieve symptoms of certain mental health conditions. Although ECT often succeeds where other treatments fail, it does not work for everyone. While it is much safer today, ECT can still cause side effects. The electrical currents are administered in a controlled setting to maximize benefits and minimize risks.

Over six weeks, I underwent twelve ECT treatments, administered twice a week. Severe depression had stripped me of all strength,

---

9 "Electroconvulsive Therapy (ECT)." *American Psychiatric Association*, www.psychiatry.org/patients-families/ect.

and my parents had to drag me out of bed for each session. I was a shadow of myself, barely speaking, feeling like I had already died. My appearance did not matter; I would shuffle out of the house barefoot, unkempt, looking like I had just rolled out of bed, staring blankly out the window as if detached from the world. My mother had to carry my shoes because I didn't even care to put them on. I prayed for something to go wrong while in the procedure, desperate for a way out of this relentless torment of my mind and soul.

Each time nurses prepared me for a procedure, I glanced around and saw older people about my grandparents' age. They were lying down in their hospital beds as IV drips started to flow. At 23 years old, I sat there wondering, *how is this my life?* Memories of my happy childhood and carefree teenage years replayed in my mind, making the harsh reality hit even harder. *Is this what my life will be from now on? Will these treatments even work? And if they do, will they be worth the cost?*

After every session, I would wake up in the recovery room disoriented, my vision blurred, with a nurse sitting by my side. I felt nauseated and exhausted—overcome by throbbing headaches. I was a living, breathing rag doll, barely existing, yet constantly experimented on—with drug after drug, and now with these treatments—all in the hope of finding something that might help me. I experienced both short-term and long-term memory loss. Back home, I would collapse into bed, wishing I would never wake up again until the next session or if at all. I did not care.

While ECT treatments can be highly effective for some, there can be both short-term and long-term side effects:

Short-Term Side Effects:

- **Memory loss:**

    Memory loss is one of the most commonly reported side effects. Some patients have trouble remembering events before or after the procedure. Some may have difficulty recalling specific memories from the past.

- **Confusion:**

  During and immediately after the procedure, people may feel disoriented or confused for a short period. The confusion usually improves within a few hours.

- **Headaches:**

  Some people report headaches following an ECT session.

- **Nausea:**

  Occasional nausea can occur as a result of the anesthesia or muscle relaxants used during the procedure.

- **Fatigue:**

  Some individuals may feel tired or groggy following the procedure.

Long-Term Side Effects:

- **Memory Issues:**

  While some short-term memory is expected, long-term memory impairments are less common but can occur, especially in those who receive frequent ECT.

- **Persistent Fatigue or Discomfort:**

  While most people feel better after ECT, some may experience ongoing fatigue or discomfort in the days following treatment, though it generally decreases with time.

- **Cognitive Decline:**

  Some individuals may experience a subtle, long-lasting impact on their ability to think clearly, concentrate, or process information.

The ECT treatments did help to lift the severe depression and constant suicidal ideation that haunted me. But to this day, I still cannot remember particular events, conversations, or in-depth details of my past. Due to the severity of my mood disorder, the benefits of this treatment outweighed the side effects, especially after other treatments failed to work.

There are other brain stimulation treatments available for depression that have not responded to traditional therapies, such as Transcranial Magnetic Stimulation (TMS). While TMS can be effective for some, it is often not as powerful as ECT for treating very severe mental illness. Unlike ECT, TMS does not induce a seizure, and the patient remains awake during the noninvasive procedure. Another option is Vagus Nerve Stimulation (VNS), initially developed for seizure disorders but also used for treatment-resistant depression. VNS involves implanting a small electrical pulse generator under the skin of the chest, which sends intermittent electrical signals to the vagus nerve in the neck. However, VNS can take several months to show results, which makes it less suitable for acute, severe depression. For more information on ECT, TMS, or VNS, visit the American Psychiatric Association.[10]

My mother, who accompanied me to every ECT procedure and diligently tracked my mood and any side effects, wrote the following journal entries:

Journal, February 15, 2001

Here I am, Lord, in the family outpatient waiting room. The hospital has become second nature for us over the past 2 years. She is having her 4th ECT treatment. We are seeing some progress. Praise your name, and I mean that with all of my heart. I know there will still be a long road ahead of us. She has so much to catch up on, and the memory loss is noticeable to me. She is in good spirits, though.

---

10 American Psychiatric Association. *Psychiatry.org*. 2024, https://www.psychiatry.org/.

Journal, March 20, 2001

*My Dearest Lord, this is treatment #11. There is such a big dif-
ference; only you can be praised and thanked. I give you all the
glory. Possibly one more treatment? Thank you for safety so far,
and I pray for safety today. Jess is different. She seems to have lost
all interest in her music. I thought that is what you had chosen for
her ministry. Help me to guide her in the right direction. Lord,
I believe that Jesslyn's recovery is a total miracle. Thank you for
being the God of miracles.*

Journal, February 25, 2002

*Dear Lord, Please protect our daughter, and thank you for her
protection and strength so far. Her improvement is a miracle by
your hand, and I give you all the power, honor, and glory. She has
a few memory problems and still does not seem to have the energy
to resume normal activity. We went to church and Sunday School
yesterday, and everyone was so excited to see her again. She had not
been to church since Thanksgiving.*

None of us can fully understand His mysterious plan for our lives.
What I do know is that God has been planning our deliverance from
the beginning of time. The Christian life is often marked by trials and
waiting. Sometimes, it feels like we will never make it to the other
side, and sometimes, that wait stretches for years—decades, even. Joseph waited 13 years for his suffering to be redeemed; Abraham and
Sarah waited 25 years for the birth of their promised son, Isaac; Moses
waited 40 years before leading the Israelites out of Egyptian captivity;
David waited around 15 years before becoming king. Even Jesus waited thirty years before beginning His ministry. Patience requires both
long-suffering and perseverance.

Hebrews 10:36 reminds us: "You need to persevere so that when
you have done the will of God, you will receive what he has promised." Ultimately, we must accept that the timing is His, not ours, that
governs our journey.

When I finally learned to trust His will and plan for my life, I found the inner peace I desperately needed. "Be still before the Lord and wait patiently for him…" (Psalm 37:7). This verse teaches us to be patient, trust in His timing, and focus on His justice rather than becoming frustrated when others seem to be thriving while we are at a standstill.

Living with bipolar disorder is an ongoing journey, and the trials it brings can be excruciating. We often expect the Lord to protect us from all hardship, but suffering is part of the Christian life. I had to learn that I could not live with bipolar disorder without Jesus. Medication can help, but it is not a cure. While it provides relief, Jesus offers refuge and rescue. When God allows things to dry up in your life, He is urging you to move to a different location—move to a different place of faith. Until we learn to move with faith, we will never see clearly. God wants us to rely on His strength, not our own. In times of adversity, we must place our hope and trust in Him, even when the pain feels unbearable. Life will present challenges designed to test and shake our beliefs. The kingdom of Satan will attempt to kill, steal, and destroy, feeding us with negative emotions that make us feel hopeless and helpless. Our tears may be filled with anger, but God the Father is not overwhelmed by our messy lives, nor is He surprised by them.

Peter writes to a group of Christians scattered across various regions, encouraging them to find hope and strength in their faith amid persecution and hardship. He reassures them: "In all this you greatly rejoice, though now for a little while you may have had to suffer grief in all kinds of trials. These have come so that the proven genuineness of your faith–of greater worth than gold, which perishes even though refined by fire–may result in praise, glory, and honor when Jesus Christ is revealed" (1 Peter 1:6-7).

It is hard to see the purpose amid the pain in our suffering. Yet, our trials, like fire refining gold, strengthen our minds in Christ and, in His timing, can shine for His will and glory.

The only person who can make your darkest demons flee is the One waiting for you on the other side. In all our despair and restlessness, we must anchor our lives in His truth and keep pressing to discover what He designed specifically for us. We must look beyond our current pain and never quit. Use hope to fuel your perseverance so you will be empty no more.

I know for me to fight living with bipolar disorder, I had to have a total heart transformation of seeking His unconditional love every single day of my life. I had to understand that He sets the course of the wind, calls every star by name, covers the sky in clouds, and strikes down the darkness that plagues your soul and brings you back to life! The Lord sustains those who come to Him! You must know that only He has the strength to do this type of work. Only He died on the cross for you and me at Calvary so we could have life. We must cry out to Him like Jonah finally did and choose submission. When Jonah humbled himself and cried out to the Lord for deliverance, this was his prayer:

In my distress, I called to the Lord,

and he answered me.

From deep in the realm of the dead I

called for help,

and you listened to my cry.

You hurled me into the depths,

into the very heart of the seas,

and the current swirled about me;

all your waves and breakers

swept over me.

I said, 'I have been banished

from your sight:

yet I will look again

toward your holy temple.'

The engulfing waters threatened me,

the deep surrounded me:

seaweed was wrapped around my

head.

To the roots of the mountains I sank down;

the earth beneath barred me in forever.

But you, Lord my God,

brought my life up from the pit.

When my life was ebbing away,

I remembered you, Lord,

and my prayer rose to you,

to your holy temple.

Those who cling to worthless idols

turn away from God's love for them.

But I, with shouts of grateful praise,

will sacrifice to you.

What I have vowed

I will make good.

I will say, 'Salvation comes from the Lord' (Jonah 2:1-10).

CHAPTER 5

THE OUTCAST

"Whoever comes to me I will never drive away."
—John 6:37

The COVID-19 pandemic had a profound impact on mental health worldwide, intensifying challenges for many and worsening conditions for those already living with mental health struggles. The enforced lockdowns and social distancing measures disrupted human connection, creating a sense of isolation. Fear of illness, anxiety, grief from losing loved ones, disrupted routines, and the emotional exhaustion of healthcare workers compounded the mental health crisis. Many turned to substance abuse as a means of coping with the overwhelming stress. However, the pandemic also opened a broader dialogue about mental health, bringing this once-taboo subject into the spotlight, encouraging conversations, and prompting society to confront it more openly.

Like millions of others, I was hospitalized due to COVID. One moment in particular remains etched in my memory. A nurse came in to take my vitals and asked me to change into a hospital gown. She opened the drawer to retrieve one, but it was empty. Turning to a colleague, she asked him to bring more gowns. While the curtain to my ER room was drawn for privacy, the team member returned a few minutes later, holding a pair of freshly folded green scrubs.

The nurse frowned and said, "I asked for hospital gowns, not green scrubs. The green scrubs are for a *crazy* one a few rooms down." Her words hit me like a punch to the gut. My stomach sank. I looked at her and quietly replied, "I have often had to wear those *green scrubs* in this hospital."

For many of us living with mental illness, there are moments when we feel like outcasts in society, even within the healthcare system. Unlike those with physical ailments, we often do not receive the same compassion or understanding. Our struggles are invisible, making them harder for others to relate to compared to conditions like broken bones, cancer, or heart disease, which are visible and widely recognized. Because mental health is misunderstood and often inaccurately portrayed, it is frequently dismissed as less legitimate.

Not only is the rejection felt in societal attitudes, but in those receiving access to care. Most healthcare systems prioritize physical health, offering broader treatment options and insurance coverage for physical conditions. Meanwhile, mental health care is chronically underfunded, with limited providers, long wait times, bed shortages, and inadequate insurance coverage. These barriers leave many of us feeling overlooked and underserved, amplifying the challenges. Often, when states are short on money, allocations for addiction and mental health are on the chopping block to be cut first.

Life insurance for individuals living with mental health conditions presents several challenges, including higher premiums, potential denials, disclosure requirements, and considerations of pre-existing conditions. Additionally, the impact of suicide clauses and the stigma surrounding mental illness can complicate the process. While not all insurance companies operate this way, based on my experience, some still exhibit these barriers. However, I have also observed positive changes in the way some insurers handle mental health.

In 1 Samuel 17:43, Goliath mocks David, saying, "Am I a dog, that you come to me with sticks?..." The Philistine giant's words reflect his disbelief and disdain, attempting to belittle David and make him feel insignificant, even laughable.

Joking about someone with a mental health condition is similarly ignorant. While humor can sometimes serve as a defense mechanism to avoid uncomfortable topics, it is never appropriate to make light of someone who struggles with their mental health. People want to be accepted and seen, not ridiculed. Mental health is a serious matter, and a careless comment could push someone to their breaking point, especially on a difficult day. Despite the media portrayal of mental health, we educate ourselves and raise awareness about the realities of mental illness. The impact of jokes about mental health can be far-reaching.

- They reinforce harmful stereotypes, such as viewing people with mental illness as *crazy* or *dangerous*. Research shows that people living with mental health problems are more likely to be victims of violent crimes rather than perpetrators.
- Jokes can affect people's ability to seek the correct treatment. Eventually, people will go silent, and their condition could remain untreated.
- Jokes can make people feel hurt, ashamed, ridiculed, invalidated. No one wants to be mocked or laughed at. Joking about mental health is not helping to normalize conversations about mental health. It is only adding fuel to the fire.

We will talk more about language and stigma in a forthcoming chapter.

A Christian call to kindness would be to understand and discourage any hurtful humor. Scripture tells us

- "So in everything, do to others what you would have them do to you, for this sums up the Law and the Prophets" (Matthew 7:12).
- "The tongue has the power of life or death" (Proverbs 18:21).
- "Do not let any unwholesome talk come out of your mouths, but only what is helpful for building up others according to their needs, that it may benefit those who listen" (Ephesians 4:29).

Words and the tone of your voice have that much power. If someone lives with a mental health condition, making jokes and hateful words could have the impact of turning a situation fatal.

His heart is for the outcasts. He is more about drawing close to the heart of His people. Christ was always willing to engage with the needs of outcasts. He can pull the pain out of your past and renew your soul. I know no one more qualified. We must see that every twist and turn has a greater purpose for redemption. God repeatedly shows that He draws near to those who feel rejected or alone. He is the refuge for those society looks at differently. I am what you could call an *ultimate advocate* for mental health. Jesus is the *ultimate advocate* for the outcasts. Even when the world rejects you, God sees you. "Are not five sparrows sold for two pennies? Yet not one of them is forgotten by God" (Luke 12:6).

He chooses the unlikely to fulfill His plans. When the prophet Samuel appointed one of Jesse's sons king, David was not invited to the gathering. Have you ever been uninvited, unfollowed, excluded, or ignored by people before? Misunderstood because you had to cancel plans at the last minute? Being left out of group activities or conversations? Feeling like the outsider in the room because of your beliefs, your skin color, the illness, or a disability that you live with? Feeling bullied or gossiped about? Being overlooked for contributions or accomplishments in the workplace or classroom? Feeling undervalued despite hard work and dedication? Being rejected hurts.

The future second king of Israel was not considered; he was overlooked. David was a sheep herder. Not seen in the same light as his other brothers. His Father, Jesse, only mentioned David after Samuel had rejected all the other seven brothers. "'There is still the youngest,' Jesse answered. 'He is tending the sheep'" (1 Samuel 16:11). David's faith and heart mattered more to God than his outward appearance. God looks at the heart; man looks at the flesh. But the Lord said to Samuel, "Do not consider his appearance or his height, for I have rejected him. The Lord does not look at the things people look at. People look at the outward appearance, but the Lord looks at the heart" (1 Samuel 16:7).

My rejection made me question His presence and feel unworthy of His love. How do we overcome the feeling of rejection?

- Do not suppress your emotions. Allow yourself to feel and process the emotion.
- Talk to someone you trust—a brother or sister in Christ, trusted family, friends, or a counselor.
- Read Scripture. "The Lord is close to the brokenhearted and saves those who are crushed in spirit" (Psalm 34:18).
- Develop coping skills like journaling, exercise, activities, or hobbies that bring joy.
- Recognize that many times, when someone makes you feel this way, it is more about the situation or that person than about your worth.

Another story of rejection that we can reflect on in the Bible is the story of Jesus. He was despised and rejected by men and ultimately bore the weight of our sins. He experienced rejection throughout His entire ministry. Because of this, He can empathize with you! He knows these feelings. Jesus was rejected in His hometown of Nazareth. At one point, He was accepted by those in His hometown. They listened and were amazed by His teachings. Then, one Sabbath day came, and He did as usual and went to the synagogue, as was the custom. He stood and took the scroll of the prophet Isaiah. As He unrolled it, He read these words:

The Spirit of the Lord is on me,

Because He has anointed me

To proclaim good news to the poor.

He has sent me to proclaim freedom

for the prisoners and recovery of sight for the blind,

to set the oppressed free, to proclaim the year of the Lord's favor.

He rolled up the scroll and went to sit down with all eyes fixed on Him. Their admiration for Jesus quickly turned to anger when he claimed to fulfill Isaiah's prophecy about the Messiah and suggested that His mission extended to Gentiles.

They rejected him, saying, "Isn't this Joseph's son?" All the people in the synagogue were furious when they heard these words. "They got up, drove him out of the town, and took him to the brow of the hill on which the town was built, to throw him off the cliff. But he walked right through the crowd and went on his way (Luke 4:16-29).

We live in a small rural North Carolina town with a population of 7,561 as of 2023. Living with bipolar disorder, I have often found myself relating to how Jesus must have felt when rejected or misunderstood. My family and I have experienced this in various settings—at school, with other parents, through interactions with my children's friends, in the workplace, and even among brothers and sisters in Christ. I may have been accepted by these people at one time, but a situation arose where assumptions were made, and no one took the time to truly understand. I often had no energy to explain or defend myself because everything else was overwhelming.

My journey with mental illness has impacted my daughters. Sometimes, my struggles made life more challenging for them—sometimes costing them friendships. They stood by me, defending their mom when other kids started to talk or make fun of the fact that I slept a lot and, at times, could hear me crying from the bathroom. Unfortunately, this often led to lost friendships for them, not just with their peers but also with their parents, who did not understand our situation.

Jesus faced the ultimate rejection during His crucifixion. No one's rejection stands against the sacrifice Jesus made for each of us. He was mocked, spat upon, insulted, ridiculed by Roman soldiers, religious leaders, elders, and even one of the criminals being crucified beside Jesus. Scripture tells us they said in Luke 23:39: "Aren't you the Messiah? Save yourself and us!" The other criminal who hung on the other side rebuked Him and said: "Don't you fear God, since you are under the same sentence? We are punished justly, for we are getting what our deeds deserve. But this man did nothing wrong." The only person who never deserved to be crucified was Jesus. Jesus answered, "Truly I tell you, today you will be with me in paradise." Jesus bore the weight of humanity's sin and experienced the maximum rejection of us all. His suffering and rejection made it possible to be reconciled with Christ. One of the very first Bible verses I learned was John 3:16: "For God so loved the world that he gave his only begotten son, that whoever believes in him should not perish but have eternal life."

Jesus understands what it means to be despised and rejected. The *outcast* can find comfort and strength in knowing Him.

A hymn that reflects themes of grace, inclusion, and reaching out to the outcast is *Come Unto Me, Ye Weary* by William C. Dix.[11] This hymn speaks to those burdened, weary, and marginalized, offering comfort through the invitation of Jesus. Here are the lyrics:

Come Unto Me, Ye Weary

Come unto Me, ye weary,

and I will give you rest.

O blessèd voice of Jesus,

which comes to hearts oppressed!

It tells of all God's pardon,

It tells of benediction,

of pardon, grace, and peace,

of joy that hath no ending,

of love which cannot cease.

Come unto Me, dear wanderers,

and I will give you light.

O loving voice of Jesus,

which comes to cheer the night!

---

11 Dix, William C. "Come Unto Me, Ye Weary" *Hymnal of the Church of England*, Oxford University Press, 1876

Our hearts were filled with sadness,
and we had lost our way,
but thou hast brought us gladness
and songs at break of day.

Come unto Me, ye fainting,
and I will give you life.
O cheering voice of Jesus,
which comes to aid our strife!
The foe is stern and eager,
the fight is fierce and long,
but thou hast made us mighty,
and stronger than the strong.

And whosoever cometh
I will not cast him out.
O patient love of Jesus,
which drives away our doubt,
which, though we be unworthy
of love so great and free,
invites us very sinners
to come, dear Lord, to thee!

CHAPTER 6

BIPOLAR BONDAGE

*"For many bipolar patients, the dark cloud of the illness is leavened
by silver linings-creativity, intelligence, and drive."*
—Dr. Frederick K. Goodwin[12]

Bipolar disorder is a chronic mental illness that causes dramatic shifts
in a person's mood, energy, and ability to think clearly. Brain chemistry and the neurotransmitters involved in bipolar disorder are dopamine and norepinephrine. It is an illness that constantly attacks the mind
and the spirit. Living with bipolar disorder over the years would shake the
foundation of my beliefs, and satan always knew just how to attack. Bipolar
disorder is frequently inherited, with genetic factors accounting for approximately 80% of the condition. I was diagnosed with Bipolar I (formerly
called manic-depressive illness or manic depression).

People with bipolar disorder have high and low moods, known as
mania and depression, which differ from the typical ups and downs
most people experience. To accurately diagnose bipolar disorder, sur-
prisingly, takes years. "The average time between a person's first episode
and getting the correct diagnosis is eight years" (Duckworth 23).[13]
Gradual onset, the reluctance to seek help, and variation in symptoms
can all play a role. The advances in mental health research are helping
to shorten this time frame. Early and accurate diagnosis is essential
to managing bipolar disorder effectively and improving the quality of
life. There was a sense of relief to know what was wrong with me,

---

12 Goodwin, Frederick K., MD. *New Hope for People with Bipolar Disorder.* Three Rivers
Press, Foreword, p. ix.
13 Duckworth, Ken, MD. *You Are Not Alone.* NAMI National, Zando, 2022, p. 23.

but I also knew that another journey was beginning with the correct medications. There is no *magic pill* that will heal you. It would take years to find the right medication combination. With mental illness, one size does not fit all. We are all uniquely different, and what may work for me might not work for you. I would go through different mood stabilizer medications only to find how dreadful many of the side effects were. One of the first medications they started me on was Depakote. I struggled to cope with the amount of weight that I had gained, especially as I was already battling depression. This situation made everything feel worse, pushing me to my breaking point when I was asked to be at a friend's wedding and found I could no longer fit into the dress size that had been ordered for me. What you have to realize is that many times, medications prescribed for severe mental illness can be just as powerful as the illness itself. Some of these medications take a good 4-6 weeks before they even make a difference. Just think how maddening and grueling that has to be for people who have to try medication after medication. Finding what will work for you takes time and a lot of patience. Some people who live with bipolar disorder are not required to take medication at all. Then there are some people like me, for whom the medication helps play a vital role in making them the best version of themself.

GeneSight testing is a genetic test designed to help guide the treatment of mental health conditions by analyzing how a person's genes may affect their response to various psychiatric medications. The test looks at genes involved in the metabolism of medicines and other pathways that influence drug efficacy. While this testing can be valuable, it is essential to remember that it is only one part of the equation. Your doctor will consider several factors, including your symptoms, medical history, and how you respond to different medications.

Interestingly, the medications that work for me are listed within the green column, indicating no significant gene-drug interaction. However, there were medications I had to stop taking immediately due to severe side effects caused by significant gene-drug interaction. One such medication was Lamictal, a mood stabilizer, which triggered a rare and serious side effect—Stevens-Johnson Syndrome—a condition that caused a severe rash that covered my entire body from head to toe. This rash is a severe, potentially life-threatening reaction that causes extensive skin damage, blistering, and peeling.

Living with bipolar disorder feels like you are on a roller coaster that never stops. It breaks the world record for the longest roller coaster ride. You rise, fall, and rise again—the ride never ends. During this process, we must remember that rising and falling are continuous growth and learning processes. "Your mess can become your message".[14] Often, it is in our falling that we find our purpose and what ends up helping people the most.

Life events such as the death of a loved one, job loss, divorce, or a chronic illness can be incredibly stressful. While stress impacts everyone, those living with bipolar disorder are more vulnerable to its adverse effects. It is crucial to recognize the early signs and symptoms of anxiety before they take hold and begin to affect your mental health. You need to carefully evaluate the impact of stress, especially when living with bipolar disorder, and be careful not to take on more than you can handle. Learning to say *no* is essential. I struggle with juggling too many tasks simultaneously, but recognizing my limits is key. I found paying attention to your red flags—those early warning signs that indicate you're spiraling. If you do not make time for your wellness, you will be forced to make time for your illness. **Read that again**.

Here are some cues I have learned that show me when I need time for myself:

- I am tired all the time.
- I am easily irritable.
- I am getting sick more often.
- I constantly feel overwhelmed.
- People always surround me.
- I am go, go, go.

---

14 Lucado, Max. *You'll Get Through This*. Thomas Nelson, 2013, p. 52

- Life is not joyful anymore.
- I am always connected.
- I never say no.

Several common myths about bipolar disorder contribute to stigma and misunderstanding. Here are some myths we need to stop believing about bipolar disorder:

- **Myth: Mania is fun and happy.**

  Reality: Going for days without needing sleep, cleaning, and organizing your home all night and morning hours is not fun. Being extremely irritable, impulsive, irresponsibly spending too much money, or displaying erratic behavior is not fun. Mania can be seriously debilitating, like depression, and, for some, lead to hospitalization.

- **Myth: People with bipolar disorder cannot be successful.**

  Reality: While I have had my challenges living with bipolar disorder, I have been married to my best friend and spouse, Jason, for over 15 years. We have three beautiful girls: Isabella, Selah, and Abigail. Today, I work full-time coaching other women who live with bipolar disorder, speaking at different events to share my story, and helping to build stigma-free cultures within our faith communities. With the proper treatment, many people with bipolar disorder lead stable, productive lives and maintain their personal goals, relationships, and careers just like any other person.

- **Myth: People with bipolar disorder are unpredictable and violent.**

  Reality: People with bipolar disorder are more likely to be victims of violence rather than perpetrators. Although there are symptoms of feeling aggressive and agitated, that does not automatically make that person violent.

- **Myth: Bipolar disorder can be cured.**

  Reality: There is currently no cure for bipolar disorder. It is highly manageable with the right combination of medication, therapy, lifestyle adjustments, and support. Living with bipolar disorder is a lifelong condition and requires lifelong maintenance.

- **Myth: People with bipolar disorder fluctuate between mania and depression.**

Reality: That thought is not supported. If I am in a manic episode, it usually lasts a good week. If I fall into a depressive episode, it could last weeks at a time: months, even years. There are very defined periods for both mania and depression. I have spent more time in the great depression than the great mania.

- **Myth: Medication is the only treatment for bipolar disorder.**

  Reality: Each person is unique and different, and each person's needs and symptoms are different.

- **Myth: There is nothing you can do to help someone you love who has bipolar disorder.**

  Reality: It is only because of my support system (my husband, my family and friends, my church family, the mental health professionals, and the community) that I am here today. One of the best ways to help a loved one is to learn about the illness and treat them like a person and not their illness. Walk beside them and take action. You do not need to be a mental health professional to help another person. Often, just being there or saying nothing at all is the best medicine for their soul at that time. You took that extra step to show that you cared.

- **Myth: Living with bipolar disorder is a sign of weakness.**

  Reality: The amount of strength it takes to live with this illness cannot be undermined. Bipolar disorder is a biological and neurological condition influenced by genetic, chemical, and environmental factors. People who live with bipolar disorder are not defined by their conditions and are fully capable of growth.

- **Myth: Living with bipolar disorder you can 'snap out of it.'**

  Reality: You cannot just wave a magic wand and tell someone living with bipolar disorder to *snap out of it* or *pull yourself up by your bootstraps.* Again, it is a chronic medical condition—this is an unfair assumption and is not realistic.

Breaking down these myths is essential to creating a supportive environment where individuals feel understood, encouraged, and unafraid to seek treatment. This serious medical condition requires compassion, understanding, support, and therapy.

Receiving the diagnosis of bipolar disorder was life-changing. I struggled to accept that I had a brain-based disorder, fearing what it would mean for my life. I was terrified that I would never find stability again, that my condition might cost me job opportunities, or that if employers found out, they would believe the myths surrounding bipolar disorder due to widespread misunderstanding. I worried about relationships—whether I would get married, have children, and if I did, whether I would be a good parent. I was anxious about medication adjustments and how my body might react each time we tried a new combination. Most of all, I feared never finding solid ground again and constantly being judged. Darkness often overshadowed me, leaving me wondering if I would ever see the light again.

Over the years, I lost jobs and friends who could not understand what I was going through. I missed weddings, Christmases, birthdays, singing events, and special music—all because there were days I could not get out of bed. Some people were understanding, while others were not interested in trying to understand. Yet, through it all, there was Jesus: watching, waiting, ready for me to return to His loving arms.

Due to a lack of education about mental health, many comments were made that kept me silent for a long time. When I finally found the courage to share that I lived with bipolar disorder, some people would respond with; *You don't look like you have bipolar disorder.* When I am at work or do not know you, I might appear to be functioning like a normal individual. When the general public sees us, we are probably having a good day for the most part.

One comment that still stands out to me is when someone told me my illness was all in my head and that I was using my depression as an excuse to stay in bed. Ouch. I have even had someone suggest that my condition was a punishment for my sins. That one deserves a chapter alone! Stay tuned for Chapter 9!

Instead of hiding, feeling ashamed, or judged, I decided it was time I found my voice. I had to build the confidence and clarity to speak up for myself, share my personal story, and communicate vulnerably with another. I had to accept that I do live with a mental illness and that it is okay, no matter what the world can make you feel at times. I realized that advocating for myself and others empowered me to overcome past fears and was a component for me to stay healthy and in recovery. Once I was able to cross over that bridge, everything changed. I eventually learned that because of my lived experience, I could relate to and help another person or caregiver who was also struggling. We know the pain that no one else can understand because they have not lived it themselves. It took me years to recognize just what a gift this was.

If you live with a mental illness, the most important thing you can do is find a community that supports you for who you are. Discovering community and people who understand you is invaluable. It is priceless, and it can save lives. Take the time to educate yourself and continue learning about your illness. Consider volunteering within your community.

In 2023, I served on the National Helpline for NAMI (National Alliance for Mental Illness) for six months, providing invaluable learning experiences for personal growth and as an advocate for others living with mental health challenges. Join a local affiliate and surround yourself with others who can relate to your journey and fight alongside you. You cannot win this battle alone, and you cannot win it without Jesus. Eventually, my story became a roadmap for others who were struggling. To God be the glory!

What I have learned over the years is that having bipolar disorder does not define who I am today. You are not your illness. Your talents and skills remain intact. Creativity and bipolar disorder go hand in hand. During my manic phases, I wrote lyric after lyric, which turned into songs, journals, poems, and now, a book! Many individuals with bipolar disorder discover that their creativity helps them navigate their intense emotions and experiences.

Your most beautiful tapestry can be woven from moments of joy and pain, challenges, failures, and imperfections—creating something you never thought possible. We all have stories, but the beauty lies in weaving a tapestry full of meaning, color, and reflection, turning your ashes into something beautiful. Writing and music have always been therapeutic outlets for me. When words failed me, I could write, creating a safe space to release my emotions and work on my emotional well-being. Writing this book was part of His plan—a goal I never imagined would come to fruition.

Spirituality can be a powerful weapon when you live with bipolar disorder. Alongside the medical aspects of my illness, I also have the spiritual side, which, in my opinion, requires just as much attention, if not more. You have to train your mind that you will get through this. Of all the mindset tools and techniques I have learned, only one has never let me down—the promises and solid truths of the Bible. The world and all it offers will inevitably disappoint you, but even in my loneliest moments, I found reassurance in knowing I was enough because I had Jesus. Dig deep within your soul and use your illness to empower yourself and inspire those around you. In a previous chapter, we discussed the importance of wearing the armor of God. In addition to this spiritual armor, we must cultivate our armor for mental health. What does that look like for you? Below is a list of the mental health armor I have found helpful:

- Spiritual beliefs
- Sleep
- Medication
- Self-love
- Sunlight
- Journaling/Writing
- Worship/Music
- Diet
- Exercise

The goal is to land in the middle of your moods. To find that middle ground, so to speak. If left untreated, the symptoms usually get worse. However, with a strong lifestyle that includes self-management and a suitable treatment plan, many people live well with this condition. I have accomplished this and continue to live a very fulfilling life. You can achieve this, too!

Bipolar disorder can develop at any point in life, with the average age of onset being around 25 years. It can emerge in early childhood or as late as a person's 40s and 50s. The illness affects both men and women equally and across all ages, races, ethnicities, and social classes. More than two-thirds of people with bipolar disorder have at least one close relative with the condition or with unipolar major depression, suggesting a heritable component. According to statistics, every year, "2.6% of the U.S. population is diagnosed with bipolar disorder, with nearly 83% of cases being classified as severe" (National Alliance on Mental Illness).[15] Scientists have not discovered a single cause of bipolar disorder, but they believe that several factors may contribute, such as genetics, stress, and brain structure. The chances of developing bipolar disorder increase if a person's parents or siblings have the disorder. However, the role of genetics is not absolute.

---

15   National Alliance on Mental Illness. *Bipolar Disorder.* NAMI, www.nami.org/about-mental-illness/mental-health-conditions/bipolar-disorder/.

A person with bipolar disorder may have distinct manic or depressed states. Severe bipolar episodes or mania or depression may also include psychotic symptoms such as hallucinations or delusions. Usually, these psychotic symptoms mirror a person's extreme mood.

What is mania? To be diagnosed with bipolar disorder, a person must have experienced mania or hypomania. Hypomania is a milder form of mania that does not involve psychotic episodes. People with hypomania can often function normally in social situations or at work. While the elevated mood associated with bipolar disorder may feel appealing—especially after experiencing depression—the *high* does not remain at a comfortable or controllable level. Moods can quickly become irritable, behavior unpredictable, and judgment more impaired. During mania, many individuals act impulsively, make reckless decisions, go on spending sprees, and take unusual risks. Often, those in a manic state are unaware of the negative consequences of their actions. I once impulsively purchased a brand-new Volvo S40 despite a salary that could not support the car payments. Thanks to my dad's savvy car dealing skills, we could trade the Volvo for a vehicle within my price range.

Below is a list of mania symptoms:

- A high mood, increased energy, restlessness.
- High levels of physical and mental activity and energy.
- An inflated sense of self-esteem, also known as grandiosity.
- Increased irritability and aggression.
- Reduced need for sleep without tiring.
- Racing thoughts—it feels like your brain is in overdrive and will not shut off. You could blow a fuse at any time.
- Overreaction to stimuli.
- Increased libido, or sex drive.
- Impulsive or poor judgment, which may lead to reckless behavior.
- Being more talkative than usual, oversharing.
- Hallucinations, seeing things that are not there.

- An increase in goal-directed activity, whether socially, at school, work, or sexually.

Preventing manic episodes involves a combination of medical management, lifestyle adjustments, and proactive strategies:

- **Routine:**

  Maintain a stable sleep pattern. Changing sleep patterns can cause chemical changes that trigger mood episodes. This is an important symptom of bipolar I disorder: severe insomnia without getting tired. I try my best to get up at the same time every day and go to bed at the same time every day, including the weekends. Daily routine: meals, exercise, work, and leisure can help stabilize moods.

- **Manage Stress:**

  High levels of stress can trigger manic episodes. I have had to resign from several jobs due to the overwhelming stress they caused. Avoid stressful situations, which include people. Surround yourself with people who support you, those you trust, and who contribute to your overall well-being, rather than those who might act as triggers.

- **Goals:**

  Set realistic goals. Setting high goals can trigger a manic episode.

- **Limit Stimulants and Substance Use:**

  Do not use alcohol or illegal drugs. Not only is this dangerous to mix with taking any medication for your mental health condition, but it can exacerbate manic episodes. Limiting caffeine intake can also help.

- **Seek Support:**

  Support groups help to provide a space to share experiences and encouragement in a place where others may be going through a similar situation. It is important to educate family and friends on the symptoms that can trigger a manic episode.

- **Regular Follow-Up With Healthcare Provider:**

  Regular check-ins with a psychiatrist or therapist can help ensure treatment plans work and adjustments can be made if needed. Keep track of any side effects that your medication may be causing or that are becoming problematic. If you are hospitalized, keep track of the discharge summary and treatment plan according to your diagnosis. Bipolar depression is characterized by deep periods of sadness, hopelessness, and emotional lows. On the other side of the spectrum, you have mania or hypomania.

Below is an overview of what someone experiencing bipolar depression may go through:

- **Loss of Interest:**

  The activities that once brought you the most joy you no longer want to do, including hobbies, socializing, and work.

- **Extreme Sadness:**

  Hopelessness, emptiness, deep sadness. The emotion is persistent, and you cannot just shake it off.

- **Changes in Appetite or Weight:**

  Significant weight gain or loss due to a lack of appetite or compulsive eating.

- **Sleep Disruption:**

  Sleeping too much (hypersomnia) or having trouble sleeping (insomnia).

- **Physical Pain:**

  Some people experience physical discomfort, such as headaches, lower back pain, or digestive issues.

- **Irritability and Agitation:**

  Bipolar depression can include irritability, restlessness, and even anger.

- **Concentration:**

  Trouble focusing, remembering details, or making decisions, which can affect work or school performance.

- **Thoughts of Death or Suicide:**

  In severe cases, suicidal ideation (thoughts) can occur. Please seek immediate support and intervention if this is a concern. Call, text, or chat at 988 anytime, or visit 988lifeline.org.

Suicide is never the answer. According to the American Foundation for Suicide Prevention, over 49,476 Americans died by suicide in 2022—1 death every 11 minutes.[16] Suicidal thoughts are a symptom just like any other symptom and are no fault of anyone. No one is to blame after a suicide death. Treatment is available and can improve over time. The majority of suicide attempts are impulsive acts—94% of adults surveyed in the U.S. think suicide can be prevented.

I cannot stress enough the reality of being discharged from the hospital from a suicide attempt. The period immediately after discharge from the ER is particularly dangerous for survivors. One in ten attempts will be repeated within 10 days. Even after the first 10 days, a repeat attempt is most likely to occur within 6 months.[17]

My family took turns watching me day in and day out to make sure I was not isolating myself too much after coming home from the hospital. Someone was always home checking on me around the clock. It is vital to monitor your loved ones or friends after a suicide attempt. It is essential to inform and educate the family on the risks of

---

16 "Suicide Statistics." *American Foundation for Suicide Prevention*, www.afsp.org/suicide-statistics/.

17 *Rush Memorial Hospital: Wellness & Education.* "What to Expect: Bringing a Loved One Home after a Suicide Attempt," www.rushmemorial.com.

suicidal behavior and how you can help. Bipolar disorder, depression, eating disorders, substance use disorders, schizophrenia, and border-line personality disorders are among the highest percentage rates for suicide.

When you live with Bipolar I Disorder, these shifts can be mental-ly and physically exhausting. Depression brings a mix of physical and emotional symptoms, often inhibiting daily functioning for at least two weeks. The intensity of depression can vary, ranging from severe episodes to moderate or mild, chronic low mood known as dysthy-mia. Licensed therapist Harold Jonas explains below that rapid-cy-cling bipolar disorder "makes a person literally live life at its extreme ranges of emotions and pushes their mental and physical endurance to the brink. It's a literal rollercoaster where the emotional 'highs' are very high, and the 'lows' are dangerously low."[18] Here are the typical breakdown of the five main stages along the bipolar spectrum:

- **Bipolar I Disorder** is an illness in which people have experi-enced one or more episodes of mania. Most people diagnosed with bipolar I will have episodes of both mania and depression, though an episode of depression is not necessary for a diagnosis. To be diagnosed with bipolar I, manic or mixed episodes must last at least seven days or be so severe that they require hospi-talization. A bipolar I individual loses touch with reality and can experience bizarre behaviors and/or psychosis. An episode of psychosis is when a person has a break from reality and often involves seeing, hearing, or believing things that are not there. Early warning signs for psychosis are:

  » Trouble thinking or concentrating.
  » Suspiciousness or uneasiness with others.
  » Spending more time alone than usual.
  » A worrisome drop in grades or job performance.

---

18 Jonas, Harold. "What Do Mood Shifts Look Like?" *Medical News Today*, written by Boram Mehta, updated 27 Apr. 2023, www.medicalnewstoday.com/articles/what-do-mood-shifts-look-like.

For me, psychosis can happen if I am in a severe manic state. I have had hallucinations and delusional, paranoid thinking. There was a time I had not slept for days, and I went into our bathroom and heard the audible voices of a newscast playing. I thought Alexa was on and playing. After I checked that it was not the Alexa, I looked around, stepped out of the bathroom, and saw no one there. Bipolar I disorder is considered the most severe kind, mainly due to the manic episodes one can experience. It is essential to know that psychosis is not a disorder; it is a symptom of the condition with bipolar I disorder. A psychotic episode can be the result of a mental or physical illness, substance use, trauma, or extreme stress.

- **Bipolar II Disorder** is a subset of bipolar I disorder in which people experience depressive episodes shifting back and forth with hypomanic episodes (a less intense form of mania) but never a full manic episode. Individuals diagnosed with bipolar II do not become psychotic. They do not lose touch with reality. Bipolar II depressive episodes can be severe.
- **Cyclothymic Disorder or Cyclothymia** is a chronically unstable mood state in which people experience hypomania and mild depression for at least two years. People with cyclothymia may have brief periods of everyday mood lasting less than eight weeks.
- **Bipolar Disorder "other specified" and "unspecified"** is diagnosed when a person does not meet the criteria for bipolar I, II, or cyclothymia but has had periods of clinically significant abnormal mood elevation.
- **Rapid Cycling Bipolar Disorder** can occur with any bipolar disorder and adds complexity to managing symptoms. Rapid cycling refers to four or more mood episodes (manic, hypomanic, or depressive state) within 12 months.

Living with bipolar I disorder is a complex journey, and there is a very real enemy who seeks to destroy you because of it. He knows what buttons to push, and his ultimate goal is to break you and your life. He wants to convince you you're not strong enough to emerge from the darkness and keep you from living in the light. He aims to mislead you, steering you away from the path God has for you. But, my dear sister or brother in Christ, you must uncover him, expose his lies, and defeat him at his game. When you fall into depression, he wants you to stay there. Trust me, I know the depth of despair all too well. I went wrong countless times by pushing God away during those dark moments, allowing the enemy to win—and he did, for long periods.

Over the past 25 years, I have learned what my unique mental health toolkit consists of: strategies to take care of myself and stay proactive in my faith. Our mental health toolkits will look different because no two people are the same. But one thing remains constant: the unchanging, unwavering God we serve.

The battle of living with bipolar disorder is daily. You never know what each day will bring—spiritual warfare does not take a day off. Satan can be both the roaring lion and the sheep. Our walk needs to be intentional. "Be strong in the Lord and in his mighty power" (Ephesians 6:10) so that we can "stand against the devil's schemes" (Ephesians 6:11). He will cause you to doubt yourself and the gifts that God has given you. He seeks to destroy your whole prayer life so you feel all alone. He is a manipulator, a family destroyer, and wants you to stay and live in complete chaos of mania or depression. He constantly reminds you of your mistakes so you will not forgive yourself and move on. He is the ruler of creating anxiety, fear, and all those voices in your head telling you—*you are not going to make it.* He keeps you from your friends, from your church. He uses every opportunity to make you feel bitter about having to live with a serious mental illness. Satan will do anything to cause a wedge that destroys you and your life.

Until you are ready to let it go and trust that God will see you through–you will continue to spin your wheels. God does not want to see you suffer. He does not want an illness to rule your life. He wants you to lay it all at the feet of Jesus. We must be consistent in our prayer life, press into the Word of God, and intentionally make the time and good choices. Do not let Satan take you from the things that bring you joy.

Living with bipolar disorder brought me shame, secrecy, silence, and the weight of constant stigma. But there comes a time when the pain and suffering become too much to bear, and the only way forward is through self-care and the redeeming blood of Jesus. As the scripture says, "For you were once darkness, but now you are light in the Lord. Live as children of light" (Ephesians 5:8). God is light. Satan is darkness. When you live in the truth of God, everything else will fall into place. In moments of uncertainty, say, *I surrender all.*

The lyrics below highlight the peace, hope, and strength found by fixing our eyes on Christ rather than on life trials and challenges. This hymn, *Turn Your Eyes Upon Jesus*, by Helen Lemmel, is a reminder of the peace and transformation that can come from keeping faith at the center of life. The lyrics "and the things of earth will grow strangely dim in the light of His glory and grace" suggest that by turning our eyes on Him, our worldly concerns fade as we rely upon His love and presence.

Turn Your Eyes Upon Jesus

O soul, are you weary and troubled?

No light in the darkness, you see?

There's light for a look at the Savior,

And life more abundant and free.

Turn your eyes upon Jesus,

Look full in His wonderful face,

And the things of earth will grow strangely dim,

In the light of His glory and grace.

Thro' death into life everlasting
He passed, and we follow Him there;
Over us sin no more hath dominion
For more than conquerors, we are!

Turn your eyes upon Jesus,
Look full in His wonderful face,
And the things of earth will grow strangely dim
In the light of His glory and grace.

His word shall not fail you, He promised;
Believe Him, and all will be well;
Then, go to a world that is dying,
His perfect salvation to tell.

Turn your eyes upon Jesus,
Look full in His wonderful face,
And the things of earth will grow strangely dim
In the light of His glory and grace.[19]

---

19 Lemmel, Helen H. *Turn Your Eyes Upon Jesus.* 1918.

CHAPTER 7

TWO PEAS IN A POD

"Do not be anxious about anything, but in every situation, by prayer and petition, with thanksgiving, present your requests to God. And the peace of God, which transcends all understanding, will guard your hearts and your minds in Christ Jesus."
—Philippians 4:6-7

Anxiety is something we all experience from time to time—whether it is due to a presentation, financial struggles, family concerns, or health worries. However, clinical anxiety takes this to another level, attempting to steal your peace. It brings a fear that feels like a thief, twisting you into emotional knots. Anxiety becomes problematic when it starts to interfere with your daily life, affecting your thinking and controlling your actions. It can keep you feeling trapped, navigating unfamiliar and uncertain territory. Ultimately, anxiety arises when faced with an uncertain future and uncharted waters.

According to the Anxiety and Depression Association of America (ADAA), anxiety disorders affect millions of Americans. Experts estimate that approximately 40 million adults (19.1%) suffer from anxiety disorders.[20] These disorders include generalized anxiety disorder (GAD), panic disorder, and social anxiety disorder, among others.

Anxiety can strike unexpectedly, quickly escalating into a full-blown panic attack. Intense fear, intrusive thoughts, and a fight-or-flight response mark these attacks.

---

20 "Facts & Statistics." *Anxiety & Depression Association of America*, https://adaa.org/understanding-anxiety/facts-statistics.

Emotionally, you may experience:
- Feelings of dread or apprehension.
- Restlessness or irritability.
- Anticipating the worst and a constant sense of impending danger.
- Feeling tense and jumpy.

Physically, you may experience:
- Upset stomach, diarrhea, frequent urination.
- Ringing in the ears.
- Shortness of breath and a racing, pounding heart.
- Sweating, tremors, twitches.
- Headaches, fatigue, and insomnia.

The intensity of the attack can be so overwhelming that it may feel like you are having a heart attack.

Anxiety goes hand in hand with bipolar disorder. It is like *two peas in a pod.* The Psychiatric Times published an article called *The Anxious Bipolar Patient.* In the article, it states "Most patients who have bipolar disorder have a coexisting anxiety disorder. These include generalized anxiety disorder (GAD), social phobia, panic disorder, and PTSD. Anxiety disorders, by themselves or in combination with a mood disorder, are associated with an increased risk of suicide and psychosocial dysfunction."[21] Anxiety disorders can leave you feeling drained, confused, and frustrated. You might struggle to attend school, work, and social events. Simple tasks like feeding the dog, doing dishes, or doing homework can overwhelm you. I have had more panic attacks than I can count. I know that I cannot face my anxiety on my own. I need to rest in His embrace and rely on His constant, watchful care to soothe my anxiety and calm my fears.

While working in a purchasing role at a local packaging company, I experienced a vivid panic attack in my office. A wave of dread

---

21   Lohano, Kavital, MD. "The Anxious Bipolar Patient." *Psychiatric Times*, 6 Sept. 2011, https://www.psychiatrictimes.com/view/anxious-bipolar-patient.

washed over me, and I felt an overwhelming urge to escape to the bathroom. However, closing office doors was unusual outside of meetings or lunch, and our supply chain area was a hub of constant activity. If I left, I would have had to pass several offices, risking interactions that I could not handle at that moment. No one at work knew that I lived with bipolar disorder along with a coexisting anxiety disorder, specifically Obsessive-Compulsive Disorder (OCD), which often involves ritualized behaviors to manage anxious thoughts. I was already under a great deal of stress, and a particularly upsetting email had intensified my anxiety. I felt nervous, fearful, unable to relax, and terrified that if anyone discovered my struggles, I might lose my job.

I was immediately overwhelmed by paranoid thoughts, a feeling of firm belief that everyone around me was somehow against me. As my fear escalated, I felt tears welling up, aware that the episode was seconds from spiraling. With my hands trembling, I stood quietly to close my office door. I walked back to my desk and bent down to reach for my purse under my desk. Fumbling for my makeup bag, I anxiously opened the bottle of pills, spilling them all over the floor. I take anxiety medication as needed that is prescribed by my psychiatrist. My hands shook as I struggled to open the bottle. I picked up the phone to call my husband after he had already received a text, who answered right away:

"Get out of there, go to your car," he urged.

I was too upset, caught in the middle of a panic attack.

"Just stay on the phone with me and talk me through this," I said.

"Your job is not worth your mental health," he advocated.

My tears turned into gasps for breath, my heart pounding as if it would burst from my chest, and I began to hyperventilate.

"Breathe, baby, just breathe," Jason said gently.

Whenever a panic attack strikes, I focus on my breathing. Though breathing feels difficult, grounding techniques can make a difference.

For me, taking a deep breath, holding it for seven seconds, exhaling for seven seconds, and repeating it helps calm me. I also use the 54321 grounding technique: noticing five things I can see, four things I can touch, three things I can hear, two things I can smell, and one thing I can taste. This exercise slows me down, using my senses to reconnect with my body. Panic attacks often come on suddenly and can last 10-30 minutes. During these moments, I repeat a short verse that I am familiar with, Psalm 46:1, "God is our refuge and strength. An ever-present help in trouble." This verse brings me comfort as I navigate each episode.

Psalm 46 has been a source of inspiration for centuries, especially in times of crisis, reminding people that even when our world feels unsteady, God remains a dependable source of strength and peace. The song below brings comfort and assurance, celebrating His power and presence in times of trouble.

God is our refuge and strength,

an ever-present help in trouble.

Therefore we will not fear,

though the earth give way

and the mountains fall into the heart of the sea,

through its waters roar and foam

and the mountains quake with their surging.

There is a river whose streams make

glad the city of God,

the holy place where the Most High dwells.

God is within her, she will not fall;

God will help her at the break of day.

Nations are in uproar, kingdoms fall;

he lifts his voice, the earth melts.

The Lord Almighty is with us;

the God of Jacob is our fortress.

Come and see what the Lord has done,

the desolations she has brought on the earth.

He makes wars cease

to the end of the earth.

He breaks the bow and shatters the spear;

He burns the shields with fire,

He says, "Be still and know that I am God;

I will be exalted among the nations,

I will be exalted on the earth."

The Lord Almighty is with us;

the God of Jacob is our fortress (Psalm 46:1-11).

"Be still and know that I am God" (Psalm 46:10) can tend to lose meaning as often as we see it embroidered on mugs, stationery, and bookmarks. You need to know that God is our trustworthy source of hope–even when He seems silent, trust that the Good Shepherd is always at work. You must believe that even when God seems silent, He is never still. He is our refuge and our strength. Nothing can separate us from the love of God. The Great High Priest is for you. He will give you the power to endure. When you are having a full-blown panic attack, it is challenging to feel any peace. The anxiety washes right over you like waves crashing onto a shore. "When panic strikes, remember that the spirit God gave us does not make us timid, but gives us power, love and self-discipline" (2 Timothy 1:7). Living with a chronic anxiety disorder is a mental health and medical condition. I live with an anxiety disorder; however, I can manage my anxiety by taking care of myself and turning to God first. I lay it all at the feet of Jesus, and I direct my source of hope towards Him.

I would challenge you to memorize your favorite verse as a weapon to use when panic strikes. A short verse that you know. Find a verse you can believe in without hesitation—one you do not need to look up. Repeat it as many times as necessary to help the attack. The gates of hell will not prevail for those who call upon the name of the Lord. Nothing is beyond His ability—He can help us win the anxiety battles of the mind!

Allow His peace, comfort, and wisdom to wash over you to find hope. Try to inhale His Spirit and exhale the hope that only He can provide. As you inhale, imagine breathing in the Spirit—filling yourself with His love, peace, and purpose. Visualize His light or comfort filling every part of you. As you exhale, release any worries, doubts, or fears. Imagine them leaving your body and mind, leaving room for hope and renewed faith. Anxiety and fear are not things that come from God. Crushed spirits dry up the bones. Without action, you will die in the wilderness of anxiety. Having faith demands action. He wants us to have a sound mind. He does not want us to keep backtracking to Egypt and never get to the promised land that He has created for every one of us.

For 430 years, the Israelites were held captive by the bondage of Egypt—for example, the Israelites found themselves trapped between Pharaoh's army and the Red Sea. When you have experienced enough of His power, you can respond boldly, knowing He has you in His loving arms. Moses told the terrified Israelites not to fear and watch what God Almighty was about to do. God is still in the business of parting the Red Sea. When you can declare His power and believe that He is faithful, the source that can replace your circumstance with peace—a panic attack tries to convince you that you are not safe, but let His Word be your source of refuge and rescue.

My past repeatedly left me in bondage and slavery, overseeing any freedom at all. There is no way to walk in freedom if you keep returning to your yesterday. I would replay situations over and over in my head, and the thoughts would bring anxiety, which could lead to delusional thinking. What may seem unlikely to be true to others felt actual in my world. Situations and seasons may have you so beaten down from the storm that you have already weathered. Those walls have to come down. In accepting Jesus, you may be delivered, but that does not always mean walking in freedom. You will sing that old tune until you are willing and ready to give it ALL to God. Not only will the notes go flat, but the song never transcends because it is not coming from the Spirit of God. You will be singing from a place of fear and anxiety.

When we fail to stay connected with God and not press into His Word, we fall into a pattern of avoidance. God will never give up on us, so we need to not give up on Him. Sitting in a Roman prison, the Apostle Paul said, "...in every situation, by prayer and petition, with thanksgiving, present your requests to God" (Philippians 4:6). Paul urges believers to rely on prayer to bring peace to their hearts, knowing God is listening and actively involved in our lives.

David had anxieties about being King of Israel. Yes, the Goliath slayer also faced many days in anguish over his gripping anxieties and fears. David spent years running from King Saul, who saw him as a threat and sought to kill him. The constant danger created deep anxiety. He expressed this in Psalm 59:1-2: "Deliver me from my enemies, O God; be my fortress against those attacking me. Deliver me from evildoers and save me from those after my blood." At times, David felt God was distant and had forgotten him. In Psalm 22:1, David cries, "My God, my God, why have you forsaken me?..." I have cried those exact words. David faced opposition not only from foreign enemies but also from those close to him. The betrayal of trusted friends and advisors leads him to plead in Psalm 55:1-3, "Listen to my prayer, O God, do not ignore my plea; hear me and answer me. My thoughts trouble me, and I am distraught because of what my enemy is saying, because of the threats of the wicked, for they bring down suffering on me and assail me in their anger. My heart is in anguish within me; the terrors of death have fallen on me."

He experienced constant wickedness and violence from his nation and people. At times, he felt all alone and forgotten by God. King David was good at lamenting and pouring out these fears to God.

According to the *National Institute on Mental Health*, the most common anxiety disorders are as listed with definition:

- **Generalized Anxiety Disorder (GAD):**

  GAD produces chronic, exaggerated worrying about everyday life. This worrying can consume hours daily, making it hard to concentrate or finish daily tasks. A person with GAD may become exhausted by worry and experience headaches, tension, or nausea.

- **Social Anxiety Disorder:**

  More than shyness, this disorder causes intense fear about social interaction, often driven by irrational worries about humiliation (e.g., saying something stupid or not knowing what to say). Someone with a social anxiety disorder may not take part in conversations, contribute to class discussions, or offer their ideas and may become isolated. Panic attacks are a common reaction to anticipated or forced social interaction.

- **Panic Disorder:**

  Panic Disorder is an anxiety disorder characterized by unexpected and repeated episodes of intense fear accompanied by physical symptoms that may include chest pain, heart palpitations, shortness of breath, dizziness, or abdominal distress.

- **Phobia:**

  A phobia is a persistent, excessive, unrealistic fear of an object, person, animal, activity, or situation.[22]

Jesus warns us about anxiety in His Sermon on the Mount in Matthew 6:25-34. He tells us not to worry and to stop wasting our energy.

---

22 *National Institute of Mental Health.* "Anxiety Disorders," www.nimh.nih.gov/health/topics/anxiety-disorders.

Therefore I tell you, do not worry about your life, what you will eat or drink; or about your body, what you will wear. Is life not more than food, and the body more than clothes? Look at the birds of the air; they do not sow or reap or store away in barns, and yet your heavenly Father feeds them. Are you not much more valuable than they? Can any one of you by worrying add a single hour to your life? And why do you worry about clothes? See how the flowers of the field grow. They do not labor or spin. Yet I tell you that not even Solomon in all his splendor was dressed like one of these. If that is how God clothes the grass of the field, which is here today and tomorrow is thrown into the fire, will he not much more clothe you—you of little faith? So do not worry, saying, 'What shall we eat?' or 'What shall we drink?' or 'What shall we wear?' For the pagans run after all these things, and your heavenly Father knows that you need them. But seek first his kingdom and his righteousness, and all these things will be given to you as well. Therefore, do not worry about tomorrow, for tomorrow will worry about itself. Each day has enough trouble of its own.

You have to listen to what your mind and body are saying. Taking time for self-care when dealing with anxiety is not selfish; it is a necessary step to build resilience, calm, and clarity. Here are practical steps you can take to support your mental, emotional, and well-being:

- **Limit your caffeine, sweets, and sugar intake.**
  I love a good vanilla latte in the morning. I have to limit these to special treats and not an everyday fix. I have opted for herbal tea and water in the morning.

- **Limit your screen time at night.**

  Put screens away at least 30 minutes to an hour before bed is recommended–this is because the blue light emitted by screens (phones, tablets, laptops, etc.) can interfere with your body's production of melatonin–the hormone that regulates sleep. Your sleep and staying on a routine are paramount.

- **Set manageable goals for yourself.**

  Your life is your life. You are not in a race with anyone. Break large tasks into smaller tasks to make them more manageable. Learn to say *no*. You cannot pour from an empty cup.

- **Engage in activities that you enjoy.**

  Turning up a song to worship or listening to a favorite podcast helps me, and I do not have to think—only listen.

- **Cultivate gratitude.**

  Shift your thinking. When anxious thoughts become consuming, think about all the blessings in your life. Not what is trying to overtake your mind.

- **Limit your media consumption.**
  Overconsumption of the media can heighten anyone's anxiety. Watch in doses and set boundaries for yourself.

During a state of heightened anxiety, you need God the most. You cannot afford to push Him aside. The cost is too expensive. "Cast all your anxiety on him because he cares for you" (1 Peter 5:7). We are not meant to carry this weight of anxiety by ourselves. He invites us to bring this all to Him, big or small. He is, right now, waiting, providing us with an open invitation to seek Him. We can trust Him! He is the only One that can bring peace to our lives. We go wrong when we try to handle this alone and without God. It is okay if you have to take medication and need counseling or therapy for your anxiety. It is okay not to be okay.

Instead of dismissing or denying your fears, turn them over to God, the Great Physician. "You will keep in perfect peace those whose minds are steadfast, because they trust in you. Trust in the Lord forever, for the Lord, the Lord himself, is the Rock eternal" (Isaiah 26:3-4). Until you learn to put the whole weight of your burdens upon the One who died for us all, you will continue to wrestle with anxiety. Make the center of attention Jesus, and not yourself. He will guide you through any anxious thoughts or panic attacks. Pray. God has never failed me, with the peace and understanding that comes from crying out to Him.

In times of worry and anxiety, it is easy to feel isolated and over-whelmed. But His Word reminds us that we are not alone and that He cares deeply for us, even in our most difficult moments. The Word is powerful and offers hope and encouragement that nothing else can stand against. Still waters run through any valley, and His Word remains true through every season of your life. May the below scriptures from the book of Psalms bring comfort and remind you that God is with you. You are safe by His still waters.

"The Lord is my shepherd. I lack nothing. He makes me lie down in green pastures, he leads me beside quiet waters, he refreshes my soul. He guides me along the right paths for his name's sake. Even though I walk through the darkest valley I will fear no evil, for you are with me; your rod and your staff, they comfort me" (Psalm 23:1-4).

"Hear my cry, O God; listen to my prayer. From the ends of the earth I call to you, I call as my heart grows faint; lead me to the rock that is higher than I. For you have been my refuge, a strong tower against the foe. I long to dwell in your tent forever and take refuge in the shelter of your wings" (Psalm 61:1-4).

"Search me, God, and know my heart; test me and know my anxious thoughts" (Psalm 139:23).

"I will say of the Lord, 'He is my refuge and my fortress, my God, in whom I trust" (Psalm 91:2).

"The Lord is my light and my salvation—whom shall I fear? The Lord is the strength of my life—of whom shall I be afraid?" (Psalm 27:1).

Anxiety disorders are the most common emotional mental health condition, affecting an estimated 31.1% of U.S. adults at some time in their life.[23] How are we supposed "to be anxious for nothing...", as Paul tells us in Philippians 4:6-7? Often, it is easier said than done, right? We must understand that God's healing can include therapy

---

23 "Any Anxiety Disorder." *National Institute of Mental Health*, https://www.nimh.nih.gov/health/statistics/any-anxiety-disorder.

and medication. The Bible does not teach that mental health struggles like anxiety, depression, or other conditions are the result of a lack of faith. Jesus Himself acknowledged human suffering and encouraged compassion for those in pain. We need to focus on the solution and not the anxiety. Louie Giglio says, "Be honest with Him to shine light into your darkness."[24] Giglio encourages people to shift their mindset from dwelling on what is going wrong to trusting in His presence and purpose, which brings a sense of peace and helps individuals see challenges from a perspective of faith and resilience.

2019 was a challenging year—one that I would describe as horrific. It was marked by overwhelming anxiety, yet through it all, I am grateful that God never left my side, even in my darkest moments. I wrote these lyrics, a song titled *Silly Girl,* on one of those difficult days when the weight of anxiety made it hard to breathe, but I still felt His presence faithfully guiding me through.

Silly Girl

Silly girl

So lost in this world

Anxieties that never let her be

She hides it well

By her smile

You wouldn't tell

She wants to laugh

Until it makes her cry

She wants to be

Free from fear inside

---

24   Giglio, Louie. *Putting an X Through Anxiety.* Passion Publishing, 2017, p. 13.

Hallelujah
How can it be
That God does
Still, love me
Hallelujah
Through it all
He's still here
When I fall
Hallelujah
She sings

Silly girl
Played a fool for way too long
All these years
The pain that lingers on
Only He
Can answer her mistakes
Broken is she
And her heartaches

She wants to laugh
Until it makes her cry
She wants to be
Free from fear inside

Hallelujah
How can it be
That God does

Still, love me
Hallelujah
Through it all
He's still here
When I fall
Hallelujah
She sings

The purpose of His plan
Is not ours to figure out
Only when you trust in God
You will have no doubts

Hallelujah
How can it be
That God does
Still, love me
Hallelujah
Through it all
He's still here
When I fall
Hallelujah
She sings

Silly girl
So lost in this world[25]

---

25   Jesslyn McCutcheon. *Silly Girl*. TuneCore, 10 June 2019. YouTube, https://www.youtube.
com/watch?v=9YFCuOFSbuE.

CHAPTER 8

STIGMA

"You may shoot me with your words,
You may cut me with your eyes,
You may kill me with your hatefulness,
But still, like air, I'll rise."
—Maya Angelou[26]

I cannot count the number of times I have heard, *but you look so normal* or, *you do not look crazy* after someone learns I live with an acute mental illness. The stories we hear the least are often the ones we need to listen to the most. People are hurting, searching for someone they can trust. Yet, because of the stigma surrounding mental illness, nearly 45% of people do not seek the help that they desperately need.[27] The struggle is real. The shadow of death looms as they live in constant fear of their circumstances. Fear grips them, piercing their soul. They endure the loneliness of an illness that consumes them, too afraid to come forward or admit they need help with something beyond their control. After facing blame and discrimination, they have no choice but to retreat in silence.

We must recognize the profound impact of stigma. We often view the stigma surrounding mental illness as accurate, and none of us like being labeled or feeling indifferent. Offhand comments about those struggling with mental health often amplify the burden they already

---

26 Angelou, Maya. "Still I Rise." *And Still I Rise*, Random House, 1978.
27 Nietzel, Michael T. "Why So Many Americans Do Not Seek Professional Help for Mental Disorders." *Forbes*, 24 May 2021, https://www.forbes.com/sites/michaeltnietzel/2021/05/24/why-so-many-americans-do-not-seek-professional-help-for-mental-disorders/.

carry, pushing them further into silence. And silence is the deadliest enemy of them all. The storm they face rages around them and within, leaving them feeling like they must endure it alone. But you are not alone. There are others, like me and millions of others living with bipolar disorder, who understand and want to help.

For too long, I allowed fear to control me, and the enemy came dangerously close to defeating me. I lived in constant fear, feeling defeated and enslaved by my illness. But God has not given us a spirit of fear. As Paul writes in Romans 8:15, "The Spirit you received does not make you slaves so that you live in fear again; rather, the Spirit you received brought about your adoption to sonship. And by him, we cry, 'Abba, Father.'" I was trapped in a cage of fear, letting it overshadow my faith. We are called to walk by faith, not sight, for fear leads to failure. It can imprison us in bondage. We cannot win the battle against fear if we avoid confronting it. When others rise against you, Christ alone is your only shield and defense.

> So do not fear, for I am with you; do not be dismayed, for I am your God. I will strengthen you and help you; I will uphold you with my righteous right hand. All who rage against you will surely be ashamed and disgraced; those who oppose you will be as nothing and perish. Though you search for your enemies, you will not find them. Those who wage war against you will be nothing at all. For I am the Lord your God who takes hold of your right hand and says to you, 'Do not fear; I will help you' (Isaiah 41:10-13).

We do not have to face this alone, fear, or let our minds take the upper hand with God on our side. We do not have to let our minds control us. Our enemies will try to convince us otherwise, making us feel the challenges are too significant. They will sometimes make you feel like this is too big for you. But when surrounded and under attack, we must stand firm, remain quiet, and be still. In those moments when fear rises, like Moses told the people, "Do not be afraid. Stand firm, and you will see the deliverance the Lord will bring you today. The Egyptians you see today, you will never see again. The Lord will fight for you; you need only to be still" (Exodus 14:13-14). God instructed Moses to raise his staff and stretch out his hand over the sea to divide the water so the Israelites could go through the sea into dry ground. The sea swallowed the entire army of Pharaoh, and not one survived. When fighting a battle you do not think you can win, think again with Christ. Stand firm, declare war on doubt, and fight against those attacking you. Words hold immense power. They can inspire, or they can destroy. They can bring life or lead to silence, making us feel misunderstood and defeated.

"Likewise, the tongue is a small part of the body, but it makes great boasts. Consider what a great forest is set on fire by a small spark. The tongue also is a fire, a world of evil among the parts of the body. It corrupts the whole body, sets the whole course of one's life on fire, and is itself set on fire by hell" (James 3:5-6).

What James is telling us is that our tongues can affect massive results. Words have an impact and can cut deep and affect our emotional well-being. We need to speak words that build one another up, not tear one another down. "Do not let any unwholesome talk come out of your mouths, but only what helps build others up according to their needs, that it may benefit those who listen" (Ephesians 4:29). "Gracious words are a honeycomb, sweet to the soul and healing to the bones" (Proverbs 16:24). Encouraging one another can breed hope. Sometimes, your words can speak something or someone into existence. People often throw around language about mental health as if it is not a big deal or mock and make fun of it. For example, *she is so bipolar* or *he is so schizophrenic*. The tides are turning around the conversation about mental health. Praise God! We have come a long way, but there is much work still to be done regarding treating mental health like physical health. What we do know is that mental health is critical. Mental illness is no one's fault. Treatment and support are essential for recovery, and people and their families who are affected by mental health need hope, healing, and recovery—language matters. We need to think before we speak and not just assume. Negative attitudes and stereotypes are hurting people, not helping. We are not just *crazy* people. The more we normalize the conversation regarding mental health, the more lives can be saved. We are stronger together. We are weaker apart.

Countless misconceptions float around about what mental illness is and what it is not. You cannot just *power through* or *get over* the giant challenge of living with a serious mental illness. It is not the same thing as being depressed and down for a few days. Depression at this level can make it impossible to get out of bed for weeks, sometimes months, and even years. You lose all interest in things you once loved and isolate yourself, feeling like no one could ever understand this depth of pain. Hopelessness takes over, and it feels as though you are surrounded by darkness. As a community, we must recognize the impact of this level of suffering and understand how we can help. The truth is that mental health issues affect us all—directly or indirectly. We live in a time when ignoring or misunderstanding mental health is not an option. In 2022, the National Institute of Mental Health found that the U.S. recorded its highest-ever number of deaths by suicide.[28] There are roughly 340 people for every mental health provider in the U.S. One in five youth had a major depressive episode in the past year, yet nearly three million young people didn't receive treatment.

According to the CDC, suicide is the second leading cause of death among people aged 10-14, 25-34.[29]

God fights your battles, and He will always win. The choice to disclose your mental illness is a deeply personal one that only you can make. I choose to be vulnerable and share my experience because of

---

28   National Institute of Mental Health. "Suicide." *National Institute of Mental Health*, U.S. Department of Health and Human Services, https://www.nimh.nih.gov/health/statistics/suicide#:~:text=According%20to%20the%20Centers%20for,lives%20of%20over%20049%2C400%20people.

29   Centers for Disease Control and Prevention. "Suicide Mortality in the United States, 2021." *National Center for Health Statistics*, U.S. Department of Health and Human Services, 2023, https://www.cdc.gov/nchs/products/databriefs/db509.htm#:~:text=Suicide%20was%20the%20second%20leading,increased%20through%202022%20(3).

the stigma and what I have endured over the years. It took me over 20 years to make this decision, but once I did, I realized it was essential in maintaining long-term recovery. The feelings of shame, silence, and secrecy all had to end once and for all. Carrying these burdens for many years weighed on my soul and prevented me from becoming my best version. If you are not ready to share, that's okay; I was not prepared for a long time and was not sure I ever would be. But when the time came, sharing my story gave me the strength and confidence to hold my head high. I faced something I once thought impossible, knowing only He could dispel the darkness that plagued my soul.

People sometimes ask how I manage my illness. I live with bipolar disorder by relying on Christ, who has overcome the world. With the armies of angels at my back, I know "I can do all things through Christ, who gives me strength" (Philippians 4:13). Harmful language—like *crazy, lunatic, psycho, wacko,* or accusations of *playing the victim card*—damages self-esteem and fuels stigma. We each have a role in understanding what mental health is and is not. Each day, I put on the armor of God to fight for myself but also for those who may not understand. A woman clothed in His armor is strong, powerful, and unstoppable.

I no longer spin my wheels in fear of what others think, of side conversations that may take place, or of the looks I get when others do not understand and learn I live with bipolar disorder. My spiritual victory has come, and I know that my voice matters and I matter to God. I want to stand boldly, speaking for myself and those who cannot speak up yet.

Applying biblical truths can shape our decisions and support overall mental health. For me, this was a process I had to learn. It takes courage to be open about living with mental illness. Satan tries to undermine us, targeting our minds because that is where he can cause the most harm, seeking to destroy us and our families. But we are called to be courageous: "Be strong and courageous. Do not be afraid or terrified because of them, for the Lord your God goes with you; he will never leave you nor forsake you" (Deuteronomy 31:6). My faith gave me the strength to live this truth—His power is unshakeable, so why should I fear? "I keep my eyes always on the Lord. With Him at my right hand, I will not be shaken" (Psalm 16:8).

I learned to ask Jesus to protect me from the pain of misunderstanding and to help me focus not on the problem but on the Provider. With trust in Him, there are no limits to what we can overcome. I hope that one day, mental health conversations will be as open and accepted as physical health discussions and that those with mental illness will be treated with dignity and respect. Through my brokenness, I found beauty from ashes. I want others to know that their illness does not define them. God often chooses the least likely, the overlooked, to accomplish extraordinary things.

All my giants had to fall at the feet of the Heavenly Father. Writing and sharing my story was always part of His plan. I have divine protection, and I encourage others to recognize who their trustworthy people are: those who stand by them, who carry light through the darkest nights, and who do not just speak of love but show it through their actions.

I became a professional at wearing *the mask*. For years, I trained myself to fake it, to act like everything was fine while I was at war in my mind. I was the best at pretending, never asking for support when needed. Whether in my professional life, personal struggles, or even within the church walls, I hid my actual battles. How many battles are you hiding in your life?

My relationship with God was fractured, and His voice roared louder in church, filling the silence that echoed throughout the rest of the week. Even when I tried to push His presence away, Christ, who lives in me, found ways to draw me back through people, circumstances, and quiet, still moments. You know that voice. You can feel those moments of conviction. Your beliefs, actions, or decisions have a profound, unshakable certainty. You always have a choice to welcome Him in or turn Him away. As Scripture says: "My sheep listen to my voice; I know them and they follow me. I give them eternal life, and they shall never perish; no one will snatch them out of my hand. My Father, who has given them to me, is greater than all; none can snatch them out of my Father's hand. I and the Father are one" (John 10:27-30).

One of the most hurtful things someone has said to me is that I live with a mental illness because of my sin. Do individuals with physical ailments such as diabetes or cancer experience these illnesses as a result of their sin? Comments like this do not bridge divides; they only widen them. Such words can wound you so deeply that you may feel like you never want to return to the place that left a deep scar on your soul. If you are afraid of being misunderstood or unsupported, you might think twice about reaching out to someone. During these crucial times, hope, help, and healing are needed.

I entered advocacy not only to share my lived experience and help others but also to combat the stigma that many of us living with mental illness face. Stigma paralyzes; it can impair the mind. As Proverbs 18:2 says, "Fools find no pleasure in understanding but delight in airing their own opinions." Breaking down these barriers by educating others, fostering empathy, and promoting open conversations about mental health is essential The stigma of people with mental illness:

- **Labeling**

  People with mental health conditions may be stigmatized as *crazy, psycho, weak, unstable, violent, attention-seeking,* and *unpredictable.*

- **Discrimination**

  People can be mistreated or passed over for opportunities due to their mental health–including employment, families, social circles, healthcare, and church.

- **Misunderstanding**

  Living with mental illness is not a result of personal failure or weakness. Mental illness is a medical condition that requires proper treatment, understanding, compassion, patience, and support. Being ridiculed and misunderstood leads people to keep their challenges to themselves—this equates to not receiving the help that they need.

- **Social exclusion**

  Because of the fear and discomfort, we can avoid or choose to self-isolate because of the perceived judgment.

The reality of someone who lives with a mental illness is:

- Just a person like you.
- Multifaceted and complex.
- Going through a difficult time.
- Trying to do the best that they can.
- Have abilities and aspirations that are valuable to the world.

Becoming an advocate for mental illness has played an indispensable role in sustaining my recovery. When I stayed silent and hid my struggles, it only worsened my situation. I allowed the darkness to torment me even more. It is easy to be influenced by the world's perception of mental illness, but personal stories have the power to shift perspectives. I want to be part of the movement that breaks down these barriers. As Charles Dickens once wrote in one of his novels, "No one is useless in this world who lightens the burdens of another."[30] Often, our greatest strength lies in the very thing that once brought us to our knees. The struggle that drains us, robs us of peace, and knocks on our door relentlessly.

While movies may portray mental health, most of them fail to reflect the actual reality of living with mental illness. To truly understand, you must educate yourself and actively participate in the solution. It is easy to say you will support someone, but your actions speak louder than words. You have to be willing to learn. Just because mental health may not currently affect you does not mean it will not impact you, your family, or someone you know. Mental health does

---

30 Dickens, Charles. *Our Mutual Friend.* 1865.

not discriminate—it can affect anyone, regardless of age, race, religion, or income. Until you try to learn, you will likely fall prey to the myths and misconceptions surrounding it. We are quick to judge others without understanding their struggles. Take the word *bipolar*—it is often used to label someone as *crazy*, diminishing their abilities and worth. But some people love to make assumptions. The truth is, we live in a world where people are hurting, and what they need is compassion, not negativity or hate. Living with bipolar disorder or any severe mental illness does not mean you are incapable of leading a fulfilling life. Many brilliant and successful individuals, including Frank Sinatra, Ernest Hemingway, Ted Turner, Winston Churchill, Mariah Carey, Carrie Fisher, Demi Lovato, Jane Pauley, and Jimi Hendrix, have lived or lives with bipolar disorder.

Here are some quotes by Carrie Fisher, Winston Churchill, Emily Dickinson, and Vincent Van Gogh:

"I'm mentally ill. I can say that. It's a great part of who I am."[31] —Carrie Fisher

"If you're going through hell, keep going."[32] —Winston Churchill

"Hope is the thing with feathers that perches in the soul, and sings the tune without the words, and never stops at all."[33] —Emily Dickinson

"The more I think it over, the more I realize there is nothing more artistic than to love others."[34] —Vincent Van Gogh

The point being is, do not assume someone's worth or qualifications based on their mental health condition.

---

31 Fisher, Carrie. *Wishful Drinking*. Simon & Schuster, 2008.

32 Loftus, Geoff. "If You're Going Through Hell, Keep Going—Winston Churchill." *Forbes*, 2012, www.forbes.com/article/if-youre-going-through-hell-keep-going-winston-churchill.

33 Dickinson, Emily. "Hope Is the Thing with Feathers" (Poem 314). 1858-1865.

34 Van Gogh, Vincent. *Letter to His Brother Theo*, July 1882.

There are many misconceptions about what mental illness is and what it means to live with it. First and foremost, mental health conditions are medical conditions. They can disrupt a person's thinking, affect their ability to relate to others, alter their mood, and make daily tasks difficult to manage. It is crucial to recognize that knowledge is power when it comes to mental illness.

If you or a loved one is struggling:
- Take the initiative to educate yourself—consider taking a mental health first aid course, consult with a mental health professional, or join a support group.
- Build your relationships. Find the people who support you.
- Find what brings you joy and purpose in your life.
- Practice self-compassion. Accepting that some days will be more complex than others.
- Focus on treatment:
- Medication, therapy, exercise, hobbies, and other wellness strategies are pivotal layers of living a fulfilling life with bipolar disorder.

For businesses and the workplace environment:
- **Foster a Culture of Inclusion and Support:**

  Provide mental health awareness training to educate managers, leaders, and employees about bipolar disorder and other conditions, fostering empathy and understanding.

- **Offer Comprehensive Mental Health Benefits:**

  Ensure health plans include coverage for mental health treatment, such as appointments, medications, and psychiatry.

- **Provide Reasonable Accommodations:**

  Allow and trust your employees to work hours or remote options to accommodate energy levels and minimize stress. Allow for task prioritization and workload adjustments during high-stress periods and episodes. Encourage work-life balance.

- **Implement Clear Policies and Protections:**

  Reinforce policies that prohibit discrimination or harassment based on someone's mental health condition. Provide confidentiality and privacy when an employee discloses their condition or seeks accommodations.

- **Continuous Improvement:**

  Adjust policies and procedures based on feedback to support employees with bipolar disorder and other mental health conditions so that all employees feel valued, supported, and empowered to succeed.

There are many online support groups you can do from the comfort of your own home, and they are free. Mental illness is not a reflection of personal weakness, lack of character, or poor upbringing. For many, it's a lifelong, chronic condition. Unfortunately, mental illness is often stigmatized with stereotypes, prejudice, and discrimination. People with mental health conditions are frequently labeled as dangerous, incompetent, or weak. In reality, what is truly dangerous is the lack of access to care for those living with mental illness, especially within the criminal justice system. According to the *U.S. Department of Justice* report, below are statistics on mental illness and the criminal justice system:

- About 2 million times each year, people with serious mental illness serve jail time.
- Suicide is the leading cause of death for people held in local jails.
- 66% of women in prison reported having a history of mental illness, almost twice the percentage of men in jail.
- 70% of youth in the juvenile justice system have a diagnosable mental health condition.
- About 50,000 veterans are held in local jails. 55% report experiencing mental illness.
- Among incarcerated people with a mental health condition, non-white individuals are more likely to be held in solitary confinement, be injured, and stay longer in jail.

- 63% of people do not receive mental health treatment while incarcerated in state and federal prisons.
- 45% of people with a history of mental illness do not receive mental health treatment while held in local jails.[35]

What is dangerous is not reducing the criminal justice system involvement and increasing investments needed in our mental health care system as a whole. Our mental health care system in the United States is difficult to access. There is a workforce shortage among clinicians. We should be engaging long before someone ever gets to the crisis stage. We need to be engaging at the beginning of symptoms.

Mental health is often overlooked compared to physical health, receiving what feels like the leftovers regarding attention and resources. The disparity extends from health insurance coverage to how people are treated in hospitals. In March 2024, I was taken to the emergency room after rupturing the C-7/T-1 disc in my neck–marking my third major neck surgery since I fell down a flight of stairs in our home on Christmas of 2019. As usual, the ER was overcrowded, and I was placed in a bed in the hallway while they administered pain medication through an IV, waiting for surgery. Just a few rooms down, a 16-year-old girl was being treated for behavioral health issues. I immediately noticed the behavioral health staff standing guard outside her door. My husband and I sat in the hallway for over six hours, receiving my treatment while observing what was unfolding just a few doors away. While we did not know the specifics of her situation, it was clear what she was being treated for.

While we were in the hallway, we overheard conversations and witnessed interactions. One officer, clearly frustrated, said, *"I'm not going to sit here babysitting her all night long."* His tone was cold, devoid of empathy or compassion, as he expressed annoyance and burden. We could hear the girl's pain—her screams, her pleas, and her

---

35 U.S. *Department of Justice.* "Mental Illness and the Criminal Justice System." *National Alliance on Mental Illness*, www.nami.org/mentalhealthbythenumbers.

anger. She yelled, *"Get me out of here! Please, get me out of here!"* She begged her mother not to leave, terrified at the thought of what was going to happen next–being admitted to the behavioral health unit. The fear and hurt in her voice were undeniable.

Periodically, staff would walk by and apologize for anything distressing we had to see or hear. We assured them that we understood, but inside, we felt an overwhelming urge to help in any way we could.

The girl's cries echoed through the hall, her pain cutting through us like a knife. She seemed utterly alone, with no one on her side. Instead, a constant stream of people hovered outside her door, their presence likely adding to her distress. Before long, her mother appeared to have had enough; she left, not staying to see her daughter admitted. Her daughter's voice grew desperate, yelling, *"Don't go!"* But her mother kept walking out of the room and headed toward the exit door at the end of the hallway after passing my husband and me. The girl's cries grew louder, escalating to desperate pleas for everyone to *"get out"* and *"leave me alone!"*

From the outside, it seemed as though everyone had abandoned her. I found myself wondering if she believed in God. That night, my husband and I could not stop thinking about her. We prayed for her fervently, her pain etched into our minds. I yearned to help her, to step into that room and let her know that someone truly understood her anguish. I wanted her to see that I would meet her right where she was—your lived experience with a mental illness is a weapon in itself. When you live with mental illness, you can relate to the depth of pain. We have many excellent resources available to help combat mental health. However, it cannot provide the lived experience.

The staff's only option was to sedate her, and both my husband and I sensed it coming—it broke our hearts to witness. Soon after, they wheeled her out, her head lolling and jerking as the sedative took hold, a haunting image that would stay with us.

When someone is discharged from the hospital to recover from a mental health condition, the road to healing is often long and demands patience, compassion, and understanding. Mental health conditions are not *quick fixes*. They usually develop over the years, sometimes without the person even realizing it. Then, a life event may trigger the condition, bringing it to the surface to rear its ugly head. Severe mental illnesses—such as bipolar disorder, schizophrenia, obsessive-compulsive disorder (OCD), panic disorder, post-traumatic stress (PTSD), and borderline personality disorder, are all complex mental health conditions that require ongoing treatment and management. Recovery is a lifelong process that involves navigating the challenges of these conditions with consistent care and support. Your circle does matter and plays a vital role in this management process.

Conversations about mental health have come a long way, but we are still far from normalizing them or giving them the same priority as physical health issues. Mental health deserves to be treated with the same seriousness as physical illness—yet it often is not. As a community, we need to step in as the hands and feet of Jesus, walking alongside those who need support on their journeys. Fostering empathy, thoughtful actions, and understanding is essential for supporting mental health. We must be equipped to help, ready to guide others with resources when they seek support, and mindful of the language when speaking about those who live with mental health conditions.

The Greek word for love, *agape,* signifies a profound, selfless love that calls us to action. I hope you recognize His authority and truth in a broken world that often pushes us toward selfishness and division. The greatest commandment is to love the Lord your God with all your heart, soul, and mind, and the second is to love your neighbor as yourself (Matthew 22:37-39). As Martin Luther King Jr. famously reminded us, "Darkness cannot drive out darkness; only light can do that. Hate cannot drive out hate; only love can do that."[36] Let's be guided by love as we fight the battle between mental health and our country today.

---

36 King, Martin Luther, Jr. *Strength to Love.* Harper & Row, 1963.

Amazing Grace

Amazing grace! How sweet the sound,
That saved a wretch like me!
I once was lost, but now am found.
Was blind, but now I see

'Twas grace that taught my heart to fear,
And grace my fears relieved;
How precious did that grace appear
The hour I first believed!

The Lord hath promised good to me,
His word my hope secures;
He will my shield and portion be
As long as life endures.

When we've been there ten thousand years,
Bright shining as the sun,
We've no less days to sing God's praise
Than when we first begun.[37]

---

37 Newton, John. *Amazing Grace.* 1779.

CHAPTER 9

GREAT IS THY FAITHFULNESS

"By this everyone will know that you are my disciples,
if you love one another."
—John 13:35

Why are faith and spirituality important for people affected by mental health conditions? The truth is that most congregations do not know how to provide support. Many lack the necessary knowledge and resources to help. *In Troubled Minds: Mental Illness and the Church's Mission*, author Amy Simpson shares the results of a survey conducted among readers of *Leadership Journal* and other *Christianity Today* publications for church leaders. Of 500 responses, an overwhelming 98% reported encountering mental illness within their congregations.[38] This statistic underscores a critical reality: mental health affects everyone.

As a church, we must recognize the seriousness of mental illness, the level of distress it causes, and the challenges it poses to functioning. More importantly, a Christian is to respond with compassion by creating safe, non-judgmental environments where individuals feel supported and valued.

Scripture offers profound guidance in this mission. In 2 Corinthians 1:3-4, we are reminded: "Praise be to the God and Father of our Lord Jesus Christ, the Father of compassion and the God of all comfort, who comforts us in all our troubles so that we can comfort

---

38   Simpson, Amy. *Troubled Minds: Mental Illness and the Church's Mission.* InterVarsity Press, 2013, p. 54

those in any trouble with the comfort we ourselves receive from God." Similarly, the apostle Paul urges us in Ephesians 4:12-13 to "Equip his people for works of service, so that the body of Christ may be built up until we all reach unity in the faith and in the knowledge of the Son of God and become mature, attaining to the whole measure of the fullness of Christ."

Through faith and spiritual maturity, the church can play a transformative role in supporting those affected by mental health challenges, reflecting His love and compassion in tangible ways.

People need to know you care. They need to feel seen as individuals, not defined by their illness. The last thing we want is to turn away someone silently suffering and alone. As a church, we must acknowledge that stigma surrounding mental health is a real issue within our communities. When people feel judged, misunderstood, or afraid, they may hesitate to communicate to their faith family for help.

The church should be a refuge where everyone knows they belong—this is our purpose as the body of Christ. We must avoid giving people the unbiblical impression that Christians should not suffer or that mental illness stems from a lack of prayer or faith. Prayer is vital, but we must also recognize that mental illness is not solely a spiritual issue. It is a medical condition that requires both treatment and support.

As followers of Christ, we are called to care for others holistically: to pray, provide for needs, show kindness, and foster understanding— even toward our enemies. To truly support those with mental health challenges, we must practice empathy, not mere sympathy, and strive to create open, judgment-free communication.

Proverbs 2:2-6 reminds us of the importance of seeking wisdom and understanding: "Turning your ear to wisdom and applying your heart to understanding—indeed, if you call out for insight and cry aloud for understanding, and if you look for it as for silver and search for it as for hidden treasure, then you will understand the fear of the Lord and find the knowledge of God. For the Lord gives wisdom; from his mouth come knowledge and understanding."

By seeking wisdom and extending compassion, the church can reflect His love and offer hope to those in need.

When invited to speak at a church or event, one of the first questions I ask is, *how many people here today are impacted by mental health? It could be you, a family member, a friend, or a coworker.* Every time this question is asked, around 90% of the hands in the room are raised. For a few moments, we all look at those raised hands. No words are needed—those hands speak volumes. They show just how critical and urgent this topic is. We must become equipped to respond, know how to help, and have resources available for those who seek support.

I am not a mental health professional. Sharing my story has given me experience and a deep passion for serving others. Because of my journey and love for Jesus, I have discovered my purpose and calling. As the church, we have an incredible opportunity to impact many lives by embracing mental health and offering support within our communities.

Our mental health system in the United States is chaotic. There is not a structured system with a clear point of entry. Because the system is fractured and disjointed, we can come together in our churches and be the burden-bearing people God has called us all to be. From the beginning, "The Lord God said, 'It is not good for the man to be alone. I will make a helper suitable for him'" (Genesis 2:18). God created us to love one another. The greatest commandment is in Matthew 22:37-40: "'Love the Lord your God with all your heart and with all your soul and with all your mind.' This is the first and greatest commandment. And the second is like it: 'Love your neighbor as yourself.' All the Law and the Prophets hang on these two commandments." We need to recognize that living with a mental illness is not because of a lack of faith or because we need to pray more. We are not to condemn people who live with a mental illness or treat them any differently. Severe mental illness is a chronic illness, and it needs to be treated and recognized like any other physical illness. Just because you cannot see it does not mean people are not suffering. We need to be providing spiritual support and healing.

At the beginning of my mental health journey, this was extremely challenging. My mother wanted so badly to try and fix the situation. As a mom and a parent, it is difficult to see your daughter or son suffering. You cannot stand to see them in the pain that they are in. The harsh reality of living with a mental illness is that no one can fix you but the person living with the disorder. You have to want to fight to live a fulfilling life. There is no other way. Living with bipolar disorder or any serious mental health condition is a battle. What is our responsibility is to love as God loves us. We need to remember the fruit of the Spirit found in Galatians 5:22: "The fruit of the Spirit are love, joy, peace, forbearance, kindness, goodness, faithfulness, gentleness, and self-control." For those of you who are caretakers, hard is an understatement. I have seen mental illness destroy families, marriages, and relationships. I have also seen these relationships mended and put back together with love. As a caretaker, your job is just as hard as someone living with the illness. You need to take care of yourself in the process. If you do not take care of yourself, you will not be able to care for your loved one as needed.

There are members, visitors, brothers, and sisters sitting in church pews weekly, suffering in silence—silence equals shame. I was one of those people. Churches are meant to cultivate hope. What churches teach does impact those who struggle and their mental health care. We can do more to support mental health within the faith communities. We can recognize suffering, reveal Christ, and restore shame and guilt into transcending a person to hope and to the foundation of Christ. We do not want people falling through the cracks. Our mission is to lead people closer to Christ by embracing them with love, not shaming them away. Steps in which churches can help ensure no one feels invisible or unsupported are:

- Speak openly about mental health. Share testimonies to help and normalize conversations. Share how faith and seeking help partner together.
- Host workshops and Bible studies about mental health from a Christian perspective.

- Equip pastors, deacons, and ministry leaders to recognize signs of mental distress and have local and spiritual resources such as devotionals and books.
- Create a team or ministry within your church for mental health support—this could include Christian counselors, mental health advocates, and/or mental health coaches.
- Offer assistance (with permission) with basic needs: meals, childcare, transportation to appointments.
- Avoid '*pray it away*' or '*have more faith*' comments. Instead, focus on His grace for those who are suffering.
- Share updates on how the church actively supports mental health within their church.
- Be a stigma-free church—this shows that you support those in your church struggling with their mental health.
- Teach that mental illness is not a sign of weakness or spiritual sin; it is an actual, treatable medical condition.
- Recognize victories among those who struggle, no matter how big or small, as a part of their healing process.

Matthew 28:18-20 says, "Then Jesus came to them and said, 'All authority in heaven and earth has been given to me. Therefore go and make disciples of all nations, baptizing them in the name of the Father and of the Son and of the Holy Spirit, and teaching them to obey everything I have commanded you. And surely I am with you always, to the very end of the age.'" Living with a mental illness does not disqualify anyone from being a part of His mission. Christ has the ultimate power over everything, including mental illness. This verse reminds those struggling that peace can be found in the Lamb of God. An individual can find purpose in and through their suffering.

I have attended church my entire life—a foundation my parents placed for my brothers and me. When I first became ill at the age of 23 and was diagnosed with MDD (Major Depression Disorder) and OCD (Obsessive Compulsive Disorder), it was a very hush-hush situation. My family and I did not know what to do or what to say to anyone. We did not understand how God was working in our situation.

We did not know how to express to others the constant state of hell we were all living in. As a family, we were not prepared to have these conversations because we did not understand. I would search for His presence, cycling through anger and frustration, only to turn when the light began to fade again. Sometimes, it becomes so dark that nothing is visible anymore. Remember these four words: You are not alone. "How long, O Lord? Will you forget me forever? How long will you hide your face from me?" (Psalm 13:1). On the cross, Jesus Himself cried out, "My God, my God, why have you forsaken me?" (Matthew 27:46).

God is still very present even in the darkness. God uses these times to deepen faith, even when we do not see it. His promises are not based on feelings but on His unchanging character.

"For I am convinced that neither death nor life, neither angels nor demons, neither the present nor the future, nor any powers, neither height nor depth, nor anything else in all creation, will be able to separate us from the love of God that is in Christ Jesus our Lord" (Romans 8:38-39).

I did not love myself. I hated living with a chronic mental illness. I could not understand why this was my reality.

My son, if you accept my words and store up my commands within you, turning your ear to wisdom and applying your heart to understanding—indeed, if you call out for insight and cry aloud for understanding, and if you look for it as for hidden treasure, then you will understand the fear of the Lord and find the knowledge of God. For the Lord gives wisdom; from His mouth comes knowledge and understanding (Proverbs 2:1-6).

Instead of succumbing to hatred or despair, these verses urged me to seek wisdom and understanding, knowing that His promises would eventually lead me to greater clarity and peace.

At the time, I was not loving myself in a way that honored God—I was doing the opposite. I pushed God away and often found myself out of sync with Him, in and out of a Christ-centered mindset. I was on a destructive path, consumed by self-hatred for everything I had become and was enduring. No one truly understood the depth of my pain or how great the suffering was. Before receiving the correct diagnosis, my church attendance was minimal. I was often too exhausted to get out of bed, and when I did, my behavior was erratic. My parents barely saw me even though we lived under the same roof. My family, our close friends, and Sunday school class faithfully prayed despite this.

Living with bipolar I disorder is deeply complex, especially when you are struggling. In these moments, the heart of Christian fellowship becomes paramount—being there for one another is at the core of a faith-filled life. These are the times when support is needed most. It is important not to wait until a crisis hits to seek help; instead, we need to address mental health challenges proactively before they escalate into emergencies.

Churches can serve as a haven for individuals and families grappling with mental health challenges, offering encouragement and assistance through the faith community. By ensuring that personal struggles are met with respect, privacy, and compassion, churches can create an environment where people feel safe to share their burdens. Encouraging honesty without judgment or unsolicited advice makes individuals feel heard because sometimes, listening is the most influential act of love.

In life's most desperate moments, it is essential to have a community of love and support. Isolation is not the answer—we were created for connection, not loneliness. As 1 Thessalonians 5:12-24 reminds us, we are called to live in peace and support one another. It says, "... encourage the disheartened, help the weak, be patient with everyone... Rejoice always, pray continually, give thanks in all circumstances; for this is God's will for you in Christ Jesus."

Through encouragement, patience, and intentional care, the church can be a beacon of hope and a place of refuge, showing the love of Christ to those in need.

Being spiritually engaged has the power of transformation. Good Christian people can still lose heart. God does not promise we will not suffer through trials and tribulations. But what He does promise is that He is right there with you. I was in training. He wanted me to know more of Him and think less of me. "He must become greater; I must become less" (John 3:30). There were times I could not see because of the deep-seated pain. Praying for another can save a soul, whether they realize it at the time or not. There were many times it was only because of the prayers of others that I could keep going. As James 5:16 encourages: "...pray for each other so that you may be healed."

When someone comes to you about their mental health, you need to know how to be there for that person. One of the most important things you can do is apply active listening skills. We need compassion. Please do not assume you know what they mean. When listening, avoid saying, *"I know how you feel, or I went through that too."* Let that person tell you. If you are talking more than 25% of the time, you are talking too much. Let them speak. Refrain from speaking too soon or interrupting them. Observe the situation and treat each person as unique and valuable. "My dear brothers and sisters, take note of this: Everyone should be quick to listen, slow to speak and slow to become angry" (James 1:19).

Encouraging and walking alongside another with a mental illness requires empathy, patience, and active support. Here are ways in which we can encourage one another:

- **Your presence:**
  Sometimes, words are not even necessary. You being there to listen is all that person needs.

- **Educate yourself on mental illness and the different mental health conditions:**
  Do not tell them what they need to do—listen and wait for them to guide the conversation on what they need. Do not try to diagnose them if you are not a mental health professional,

such as a psychiatrist, psychologist, physician assistant, or other mental health counselor.

- **Keep checking in:**
  A simple text, email, or phone call can make a person feel not so alone.

- **Be forgiving of last-minute canceled plans, mood swings, or periods of withdrawal.**

- **Encourage them to join a support group, a church Bible study, or to get involved with their community.**

- **Stand up for them if you hear people speaking negatively about their behavior behind closed doors–you need to be an advocate for them.**

- **Be mindful of their boundaries.**

Whether this requires their personal space or they are not ready to open up about specific topics yet. They will open up when they are ready.

The church needs to understand and embrace the idea that, in many cases, medication is a necessary and effective tool for treating mental health conditions. Here is how the church can approach this with compassion and biblical understanding:

Just as physical illnesses like diabetes or high blood pressure require medication, mental health conditions often have biological and chemical components that require the need for medication.

- Not everyone's road to recovery will require medication. Each journey is uniquely different. Respect that each path taken will never look the same from one individual to the next.
- God cares about the whole person, the mind, body, and spirit. Teaching that medication is a tool that God uses for healing can help the church embrace the reality of mental health care.
- People should never fear criticism or misunderstanding about taking medication to improve themselves. Medication is not a

cure, but it can help stabilize someone and get them back on their feet."

Mental health affects everyone and according to *National Alliance on Mental Illness,* "1 in 5 U.S. adults experience mental illness each year."[39] Although we have come a long way, we are not doing enough. A day does not go by without hearing of another tragic loss due to mental illness. Early intervention is key. People affected by mental health conditions and their families and caregivers need help, hope, and healing. Mental illness can, for some, cause feelings of spiritual isolation. They do not occur due to a lack of faith. You can be a deeply spiritual person and still experience depression or live with a mental health condition. People and families caught in the turmoil of being surrounded by mental illness can feel lonely and isolated. For our family, whose lifeline has always been the church, we were never so alone. Your church is supposed to be your safe place, but we did not know how to speak up about the chaos we were all living in. We all feared speaking up and people not understanding. Faith communities are among the first places people turn to in a crisis. We need to have resources and information available when needed. Our churches need to embrace seeing a person who lives with a mental health condition. We need to embrace all people in the same way, regardless of the disability or illness they may be living with.

People never forget those who bring them a torch in the middle of all the darkness. Moments that I have never forgotten occurred in times such as this. A particular pastor came to my parents' house in my early twenties. He noticed I had not been to church in a few months and decided to stop by with permission. Somehow, he convinced and encouraged me to go downstairs and have a conversation. We talked for hours, and he sat beside me and prayed. Small acts of kindness like bringing a meal or my pastor stopping by, again, with permission are never forgotten and go a long way. You cannot be offended if the person is suddenly no longer up for a conversation, and you may be

39 National Alliance on Mental Illness. *Mental Health by the Numbers.* NAMI, https://www. nami.org/about-mental-illness/mental-health-by-the-numbers/.

asked to leave—this is a process. Respect any privacy needed. If that person is not ready to be seen or feels like talking, and you brought a meal, leave it on their doorstep and send a quick text telling them. We feed those in our congregations who are experiencing physical illness all the time. Caring for a disorder from the neck up should not be treated differently. Just like physical illness can confine you to a bed for healing, depression can confine you to a bed until you feel better.

I will never forget the cards and flowers sent, most importantly, the prayers when I could not even pray for myself. I was being lifted and protected by these prayers. I had a constant prayer wall of protection. Do not underestimate the power of prayer! Those prayers held me up when I did not have the strength to do it. In 1 Corinthians 13:13 says, "And now these three remain: faith, hope and love. But the greatest of these is love." You may not realize how impactful a simple action, like sending a card during times of despair, can be. I will keep this card forever that I once received when the darkness consumed my soul. On the front of the card, it said *"Feel Better"* with a bouquet and a bandaid with a heart wrapped around the flowers to keep them held together. On the inside of the card, it said, *"Sending healing thoughts your way."* What was written will stay with me forever.

> *"Oh, sweet girl, I wish I could take over your illness and allow you to run carefree with your family. I wish I could set your mind free. I have had a good life. I am older and want a great life for you, Jason, and your beautiful girls. You are stronger than you know because God gave you this family. He placed the voice of an angel within you, and you have used it to bless so many of us. I don't know why I took such a liking to you, but please know I am and will help you in ANY way! I can hold your hand, smile, cook, and always remind you that you are loved—but you already know that you are special! I love you. Your friend, Cathy.*

Since millions of people are affected by mental illness each year, the likelihood of them sitting in the pew next to you is high. Did you know that these people can even be our pastors? Many faith leaders have a 24/7 mentality that they cannot turn off. They do not know when the next call, text, or criticism will come. We have these expectations from our church leaders that can wear and tear on them and affect them spiritually. Dr. Tim Clinton and Dr. Jared Pingleton from the *American Association of Christian Counseling* shared that 90% of pastors work more than 50 hours weekly.[40] Burnout is often the leading cause of depression and anxiety among pastors today. We need to foster empathy and compassion when it comes to mental health. God created the entirety of man: body, soul, spirit, and MIND—each part designed to function as a whole. Seeking help is providing the nourishment and support that our minds need. Christians are not superhuman. We are flawed and broken, and in situations concerning mental illness, sometimes it takes seeing a licensed professional and taking medication.

We work to bridge the divide. We must recognize the tools available to churches and share this knowledge with others. We must give ourselves grace and understand that we cannot navigate this journey alone. By sharing hope, we open the door for transformation—anything is possible, and change can happen. We need to run this race together, supporting one another every step of the way. It is not enough to approach each other in need; we should walk alongside one another through every challenge. When we begin to share openly, the walls of shame and fear are slowly dismantled, piece by piece. Above all, we must become faith communities open to discussing mental health in light of our faith. If Jesus was concerned with the well-being of our minds and hearts, shouldn't our churches be, too?

Mental illness is not going away. Our country is in a state of a mental health crisis, with people hurting and needing the help that they so desperately deserve. Year after year, the statistics are higher.[41] In North Carolina alone, 1,469,000 adults have a mental health con-

---

40   Clinton, Tim, and Jared Pingleton. *The Struggle Is Real: How to Care for Mental and Relational Health Needs in the Church.* WestBow Press, 21 Sept. 2017, p. 81

41   National Alliance on Mental Illness. *Mental Health Policy Stats.* NAMI, https://nami.quorum.us/mhpolicystats/.

dition. That is more than three times the population of Raleigh. In North Carolina, 356,000 adults have a serious mental illness. We deserve to be seen as a whole person. Seeking help is providing the nourishment and support that our minds need.

How the church treats those with mental health conditions is crucial to the feeling of security. Suppose you are afraid of being misunderstood or unsupported. In that case, you might think twice about reaching out to your faith community, which is especially important when health and healing are desperately needed. Jeremiah, the weeping prophet, faced rejection, persecution, and loneliness as he delivered His message to rebellious people. He was not only mocked and ridiculed by the people of Judah but also profoundly misunderstood. As a result, he felt alone in his calling, with no one to support or encourage him. He was left spiritually drained. He says in Lamentations 3:1-3, "I am the man who has seen affliction by the rod of the Lord's wrath. He has driven me away and made me walk in darkness rather than light; indeed, he has turned His hand against me again and again, all day long." He felt as though his life had no value in the constant rejection and hardship. In Jeremiah 9:1, he expresses how deeply he wished for relief from his burden: "Oh, that my head were a spring of water and my eyes a fountain of tears! I would weep day and night for the slain of my people." While Jeremiah's emotional struggles were very real, God never abandoned him. He reminded him that He still had a plan for him. His faithfulness was an anchor to Jeremiah despite the overwhelming odds. Jeremiah's example shows that it is possible to be profoundly faithful yet experience emotional and mental pain. It highlights how God offers peace even within the darkness.

Having a mental illness can radically affect our faith and how we practice it. I will admit there were times when I was angry at God. I could not understand why I was not getting better or why I had to keep enduring one valley after another. In the first three years leading up to my bipolar I disorder diagnosis, my family and I lived in constant turmoil, never knowing if I would make it through another day. Eventually, my parents left the church for a season because they could no longer answer the same questions week after week about my progress—there was never any. My mother could not attend church without fighting back tears or crying. We need to change this reality. We must create an environment where people feel safe to disclose their mental health struggles so they are not pushed away from the very place they need the most. The church should be a sanctuary, not a source of isolation. I hope that one day, mental illness will be fully normalized—free from stigma, myths, and misunderstanding. I dream of a time when individuals with mental illness no longer feel, through their interactions with the church, that they are rejected by God or beyond help and healing. The truth is, there is always hope. The church holds a unique opportunity to play a vital role in the continuum of care for mental health—an essential role that remains absent in many faith communities today. By embracing this responsibility, the church can reflect His love and become a haven of hope, healing, and acceptance.

Great is Thy Faithfulness

Great is Thy faithfulness, O God my Father,

There is no shadow of turning with Thee;

Thou changest not, Thy compassions, they fail not,

As Thou hast been, Thou forever wilt be.

Great is Thy faithfulness! Great is Thy faithfulness!

Morning by morning new mercies I see;

All I have needed Thy hand hath provided—

Great is Thy faithfulness, Lord, unto me!

Summer and winter and springtime and harvest,

Sun, moon, and stars in their courses above,

Join with all nature in manifold witness

To Thy great faithfulness, mercy, and love.

Great is Thy faithfulness! Great is Thy faithfulness!
Morning by morning new mercies I see;
All I have needed Thy hand hath provided—
Great is Thy faithfulness, Lord, unto me!

Pardon for sin and a peace that endureth,
Thy own dear presence to cheer and to guide;
Strength for today and bright hope for tomorrow,
Blessings all mine, with ten thousand beside!

Great is Thy faithfulness! Great is Thy faithfulness!
Morning by morning new mercies I see;
All I have needed Thy hand hath provided—
Great is Thy faithfulness, Lord, unto me![42]

---

42   Chisholm, Thomas O. *Great Is Thy Faithfulness*. 1923.

CHAPTER 10

DO NOT LET ME GO

"Though the fig tree does not bud and there are no grapes on the vines, though the olive crop fails and the fields produce no food, though there are no sheep in the pen and no cattle in the stalls, yet I will rejoice in the Lord, I will be joyful in God my Savior"
Habakkuk 3:17-18

In life, sometimes you have to break before you see God and understand the plan He has for your life. You must discover a reason to keep going, one bigger than yourself. This chapter will be heavy to write. 2019 haunted me like a twisted nightmare for a very long time. I had relapsed. Badly. This year was not good. It was a year of intense struggle. I felt bound, like a prisoner to my despair. From February to October 2019, I was held captive by my circumstances. My life came crashing down, and in that wreckage, I was on my knees wailing, begging, pleading for His hand to come upon me. *Do not let us go. Do not let me go.*

In December of 2018, I was working as a Regional Materials Manager for a global packaging company. My home office was in Lexington, NC, but I also frequently traveled to the Greensboro plant throughout the week. My work weeks were grueling—50+ hours filled with constant travel and mounting stress. Each day felt like I was diving headfirst into a pool of anxiety, sinking beneath the challenges piled up.

The red flags were there, but I ignored them at first. Slowly, the signs became impossible to miss. Anxiety consumed me, and the dread of Mondays weighed heavily on my shoulders. I hated to think of facing another week of work that drained me entirely. By the time I got home each evening, I had nothing to give, not to my family, not to myself, and not to God.

Instead, my family bore the brunt of my frustration, irritability, and exhaustion. Depression crept in as the months dragged on, tightening its grip. Sleep eluded me, and the anxiety manifested physically; my eyes twitched constantly from the overwhelming stress and lack of rest. I had to escape to the restroom to have panic attacks while at work. No job is worth your mental health.

I knew something had to change, or I would be in serious trouble. Every morning felt like a battle to get out of bed. My energy was running on empty, and I dragged myself through the day, weighed down by an invisible ball and chain that clung to me like my shadow. My appetite vanished, and I rarely ate dinner. My mornings started very early. The kids and I were out the door by 6:45 a.m. every day. After enduring the grueling rush hour traffic, I would finally arrive home after 6:00 p.m., completely spent. Most nights, I barely had the strength to settle the kids in for bed. Physically and mentally drained, I would collapse into bed, dreading the thought of facing another day.

One of the greatest gifts I have in my life is my husband. 1 Corinthians 13:4-6 reminds us, "Love is patient, love is kind. It does not envy, it does not boast, it is not proud. It does not dishonor others, it is not self-seeking, it is not easily angered, it keeps no record of wrongs. Love does not delight in evil but rejoices with the truth." In 2010, I married my best friend, Jason. A man that God specifically designed for me. It would take someone with the patience of Job to walk this journey with me, especially living with the complexities of bipolar I disorder. Yet, Jason has embraced every part of who I am, loving me boldly and unconditionally for over 15 years. Every day, he meets me exactly where I am, filling my soul with laughter and my heart with reassurance. Jason has shown me endless compassion, empathy, encouragement, and acceptance as I navigate the challenges of living with a chronic mental illness. I have seen marriages shattered by the weight of mental health struggles, but I have also seen God restore and rebuild relationships. Ours is a testament to the latter.

I had been working in my position for two and a half years when Jason and I had the conversation: I could not keep doing this position. Living with mental illness teaches you to recognize and know when it is time to seek help. We decided that I would submit my resignation letter.

From the outside, no one would tell. My fake smile and well-practiced acting skills masked the turmoil inside. After years of hiding my emotions, I had become a professional at pretending everything was FINE:

The **F** stands for fatigued, falling apart, frightened, feeling low, fragile, fearful, fidgety, flat, and fading.

The **I** stands for insignificant, irritable, in pain, isolated, impatient, invisible, inadequate.

The **N** stands for nervous, numb, negative, not well, neurasthenic (emotionally disturbed).

The **E** stands for estranged, empty, exhausted, edgy, eroded.

Have you ever just felt F.I.N.E. before?

The warning signs were clear. The alarms, bells, and whistles were going off. You must take care of yourself before your mental health forces you to. Let me say that again: **you must take care of yourself before your mental health takes care of you.**

During this time, I was under the care of a nurse practitioner who had adjusted my medication to address my emergency decline. For years, I had been managing well on two medications: Wellbutrin (bupropion), an antidepressant, and Seroquel (quetiapine), an antipsychotic. However, the nurse practitioner added Cymbalta (duloxetine), another antidepressant, despite the medication having a moderate gene-drug interaction.

I have always been diligent about taking my medication as prescribed, like clockwork, at the same time every day. To stay organized, I use a pill organizer—the kind with days of the week labeled on each lid—just like the ones my dad and grandmother used for their medications. This simple tool serves as a helpful reminder and keeps me on track.

Jason worked early that morning, and my girls were sound asleep. I was the only one awake. Around 3:30 a.m., he did his usual routine. He came to my side of the bed, kissed my forehead, and checked I was okay before leaving. That morning, I told him something felt off, and I was feeling strange. Still lying down, I told him I would call if I needed him to turn around and come back home.

Fifteen minutes after he left, I tried to sit up, but something was wrong. My whole body began to shake uncontrollably. When I tried to stand, my legs lost all coordination and buckled beneath me. I reach for my phone, desperately trying to call for help. The first person I dialed was my mom, who lived just down the street. I could barely grip the phone, but I managed to call her.

When my mom pulled into the driveway, she saw me from the sidewalk, shaking violently, my body convulsing in a full-on seizure. She rushed to me, immediately calling 911.

"911, what is your emergency?"

"It is my daughter—please come quickly!"

"Calm down, ma'am. Can you tell me what is happening?"

"She is shaking uncontrollably and is now shaking everywhere, lying on the floor. We need help now!"

"Help is on the way. Stay with me until the paramedics get there."

"Mom, I don't think I'm going to make it," I whispered.

"Yes, you are. Hang on, honey. Yes, you are," she replied, her voice breaking.

By this time, I was going in and out of consciousness, my eyes rolling back, laying like a rag doll in her arms.

"Jesslyn!" my mom cried out in fear. "Jesslyn!"

I saw the panic in her eyes before mine began to shut.

She began praying over me, rocking me back and forth like she did when I was a baby.

"In the name of Jesus, please do not take her. In the name of Jesus, please do not take her!"

My body went limp, tired from the violent shaking. There was nothing left but random jerky movements. We lay there for twenty minutes that night before an ambulance was able to come. In the waiting, in the stillness, something happened. I felt a warm rush from my head to my toes and slowly opened my eyes.

"Mom?" I whispered weakly.

"Jesslyn, hang on. They will be here any minute," she reassured me, her voice filled with anxiety.

"Mom, something just happened," I said, still trying to process my feelings.

"What happened?" she asked, her voice shaking with worry.

"I have felt this warm sensation…it rushed from my head down to my toes. I do not know how to explain it, but something happened."

This did not happen just once that day; it happened two other times while in the emergency room. I could not walk for over six hours. It was the hand of God saving my life once again. All I could pray was, *do not let me go, do not let me go.*

That night, I was diagnosed with a serotonin syndrome overdose. If you take multiple medications at once, they can affect the serotonin levels in your brain. It is rare, but too much serotonin building up in your brain can be life-threatening. Serotonin is a neurotransmitter that plays a crucial role in many of the bodily functions. Low serotonin levels are often linked to conditions like anxiety and depression. Symptoms of serotonin syndrome can develop within minutes to hours of taking medications that influence serotonin levels, especially combining 2-3 different medications all at the same time. The risk is higher when you start a new medication or increase the dosage. Additionally, street drugs such as methamphetamine, cocaine, opiates, ecstasy, and LSD have also been associated with serotonin syndrome.

Here is a list of the serious side effects that I had:

- Irregular heartbeat and high blood pressure
- Seizures
- Tremors
- In and out of consciousness
- Uncontrolled muscle spasms causing severe muscle breakdown
- Abnormal eye movements
- Loss of muscle coordination

The doctors could explain all my symptoms—except one: the warm, rushing sensation that flowed from my head to my toes. It was a divine reminder that my God-given assignment was not yet complete. Whatever He was preparing me for would be beyond anything I could have imagined. But that is who our God is—turning the impossible into the possible.

For the next couple of months, I was haunted by recurring nightmares and flashbacks of that traumatic night–the ghosts of my past. I could vividly relive every moment, and the thoughts felt intrusive and relentless. The images were so distressing that they triggered severe anxiety. I would wake up in the middle of the night drenched in sweat, gasping for air, and sometimes screaming out. Jason would wake up, gently holding me, repeating, *"It is just a dream, it is just a dream, I am right here."* But it felt as though I was reliving the trauma all over again. I could not go back to sleep afterward and was always on edge, waiting for the next wave of fear. The nightmares continued to torment me, and I lived in constant dread of what had happened.

A couple of months later, I was diagnosed with PTSD (post-traumatic stress disorder). Post-traumatic stress disorder is a condition in which a person has witnessed or experienced frightening, life-threatening, or disturbing events and has recurring flashbacks, nightmares, or anxiety about the events. The episodes intrude frequently within a person's life and become debilitating. Causes of PTSD can also be from sexual assault or abuse, natural disasters, accidents or injuries to oneself or others, or being in a life-threatening situation.

Symptoms of PTSD in adults can include:
- Recurring upsetting memories
- Angry outbursts
- Substance abuse
- Distancing oneself from a loved one
- Reckless or self-destructive behaviors
- Lack of interest in favorite activities
- Avoidance of potential triggers (specific people, events, and situations)
- Violent behavior or destruction of property
- Depersonalization
- Derealization
- Exaggerated startle response
- Difficulty concentrating
- Memory issues
- Vivid and disturbing nightmares
- Hyperarousal or the opposite
- Sleep issues
- Hypervigilance
- Continual negative mood

Symptoms of PTSD in soldiers and veterans include:
- Intrusive memories or flashbacks
- Recurring nightmares
- Hypervigilance
- Intense distress or irritability
- Developing a destructive addiction

- Suicidal thoughts
- Physical reactions when remembering the trauma, including sweating, nausea, and rapid breathing
- Avoidance
- Feeling emotionally numb and detached from others
- Feeling hopeless about the future
- Inability to remember important aspects of the traumatic event
- Anxiety
- Bouts of moodiness or anger
- Insomnia

PTSD affects 3.6% of the U.S. adult population, about 9 million Americans. About 37% of those diagnosed with PTSD are classified as having severe symptoms. Women are significantly more likely to experience PTSD than men.[43]

Helping yourself and practicing self-care while experiencing PTSD is key. After I was diagnosed, I immediately went into psychotherapy to help provide grounding techniques as a relief from the symptoms I was having. Seeking emotional support was a necessity and an essential aspect of treatment during this season of my life. My family, church, and dog, Shandi, also supported me emotionally. Joining a community group or connecting with others living with PTSD can also provide help, along with being a part of or affiliated with a community of people who understand. *NAMI (National Alliance for Mental Illness)* has an excellent resource called NAMI Homefront, a program for family members of veterans and service members whose traumatic experiences are associated with military service.[44]

For months, I battled intense panic and paranoia. I stubbornly refused to take any medication, which only worsened my mental health. I remained stuck in a constant cycle of mania and depression like a

---

43 National Alliance on Mental Illness. *NAMI Homefront.* NAMI, https://www.nami.org/support-education/mental-health-education/nami-homefront/.

44 National Alliance on Mental Illness. *NAMI Homefront.* NAMI, https://www.nami.org/Support-Education/Mental-Health-Education/NAMI-Homefront/.

seesaw, teetering back and forth between the extremes. One moment, I was consumed by severe mania; the next, I sank into deep depression. During one sleepless night, overwhelmed by terror, I found myself scribbling these words on April 26, 2019 at 3:35 a.m.:

Spiritual war

Inside my head

I will not crumble

I will rise instead

Your armor on me

I am prepared to fight

Spiritual war

I am not going down tonight

Your armor's on me

I am ready to fight

Spiritual war

I am not going down tonight

For eight months straight, Satan and his army of demons relentlessly tried to bring me down daily. Nagging whispers rang in my ear: *You are done, you are finished, this time, you will fail—you are not strong enough to keep going on.* For any Michael Jackson fans, it reminded me of that wicked laugh at the end of his popular song and video for *Thriller.* Demons were closing in on every side. He thrives on condemning you, making you believe these lies. He takes pleasure in seeing you dangle by a thread, spiraling out of control. His relentless attacks surrounded me, his piercing darts hitting me from every direction. Day in and day out, he sought to destroy me one and for all. Something evil was lurking all through the dark that night.

It took six long months before my Psychiatrist finally convinced me to go back on my medication. I was not getting any better; I was only getting worse. Most of 2019 was spent in isolation, struggling to find my way back to freedom and away from the constant mood swings of mania and depression. Just when I thought I had turned the corner, December brought another setback. I fell down that same flight of stairs that led me to the terror I was gripped with for most of 2019, with my head taking a beating with each stair down. The fall caused significant injury to my neck. When I hit the ground, the impact knocked the wind out of me, leaving me unable to move or whisper a faint *help*. It was a miracle I had not broken my neck. However, I had ruptured a disc at the C-3/C-4, requiring emergency cervical fusion surgery. The pain was excruciating. Once again, I was forced into recovery, unable to work for weeks. Six months later, I faced another cervical fusion surgery at the C-5/C-6 due to a second rupture caused by the initial fall.

During this season, God invited me to know Him on a deeper level–an intimacy that could only be forged through such unwelcome trials. It was a wake-up call, and slowly, I began to see the bigger picture. Amid this hurricane, heavy and violent, He was showing me that He is still Lord of all. Through it all, I realized I had a story to tell, and He had a purpose He intended for me to fulfill. I was a branch on His vine, and He was not done with me yet. Clinging to Him, I cried: *"Abba, Father, do not let me go."*

> I waited patiently for the Lord; he turned and heard my cry.
>
> He lifted me out of the slimy pit, out of the mud and mire;
>
> He set my feet upon a rock and gave me a firm place to stand.
>
> He put a new song in my mouth, a hymn of praise to our God.
>
> Many will see and fear the Lord and put their trust in him (Psalm 40:1-3).

CHAPTER 11

JUST AS I AM

*"The areas in which you are experiencing the most adversity are the
areas in which God is at work."*
—Dr. Charles F. Stanley[45]

January 2023 changed the trajectory of my life. During a Sunday morning service, the pastor posed a powerful question: *What does the bloodstained cross mean to you, and what will you do about it?* Are you willing to give it all, as Christ did for us? He who is in me is greater than He who is in this world (1 John 4:4). I realized I was tired of being trapped in the cycle of being sick and tired. It was time to stop with all the excuses and recognize that God had a plan and a purpose for my life. No, I did not feel equipped. I thought I was not knowledgeable enough to understand what I had sensed for some time. He was urging me to shift my focus away from my illness. In Exodus, God gives Moses an assignment for which He felt unprepared.

> Moses said to the Lord, 'Pardon your servant, Lord. I have never been eloquent, neither in the past nor since you have spoken to your servant. I am slow of speech and tongue.' The Lord said to him, 'Who gave human beings their mouths? Who makes them deaf or mute? Who gives them sight or makes them blind? Is it not I, the Lord? Now go; I will help you speak and will teach you what to say' (Exodus 4:10-11).

My illness was not going to take control any longer; I was done. Suddenly, I felt a supernatural boldness rise within me—a courage

---

45 Stanley, Charles F. *How to Handle Adversity.* Thomas Nelson, 1989, p. 11.

that allowed me to let go of the fear of judgment. I no longer cared if people knew I lived with bipolar I disorder. I was ready to take off the mask and stop hiding this part of myself, refusing to feel shame for living with a chronic illness. It was time to step into my authenticity and purpose.

I immersed myself in advocacy, openly telling anyone willing to listen about my journey. You have a story, too. Whether you are living with bipolar disorder, battling cancer, or grieving the loss of a loved one, your story holds power, and it could inspire and help someone else. For years, I could not imagine how God could use my experience with a serious mental illness to make an impact. I did not think I would ever be well enough. But when I started to speak up, something amazing happened—a pivotal turning point in my healing process.

In 2020, I discovered a program called *In Our Own Voice* (IOOV) through NAMI, which offered free training. This interactive presentation is guided by two individuals living with mental health conditions and includes video, discussions, and a Q&A session. It provides a unique glimpse into what it is like to live with mental illness. This program taught me how to share my story by focusing on four key parts: an introduction, what happened, what helped me, and what is next. The process was not easy. Being that vulnerable and revisiting years of pain was incredibly challenging. However, completing the training gave me confidence even though I was not ready to speak publicly. I knew that one day, I would find the courage to find my voice.

Do you believe that you can live a fulfilled life living with a serious mental illness? Do you trust that God will provide you with a way out?

Living with bipolar I disorder is a battle. Everyday triggers can involve stress, certain medications, seasonal changes, tragic circumstances such as death, or a chronic medical condition. I pray that in addition to medically taking care of yourself as needed, you wear the belt of truth, put on the breastplate of righteousness, protect your feet with the gospel of peace, take up the shield of faith, fight with the sword of the Spirit, and protect your mind by wearing the helmet of salvation where most of the battles are either won or lost. I want you to win this war. My hope for you is that you can see from my story that our God is more than capable of making the impossible possible. He can use your experiences on a psych ward one day for His glory if you trust His goodness. Never stop fighting, lose hope, and never be ashamed of who you are. You can win this war. God does not waste wounds.

Those who dwell in the darkness and walk through the shadow of death can profoundly impact others. True freedom comes only through knowing the Truth. We must decrease so that He must increase—this requires stepping outside of self-centered thinking and beyond the limitations of our circumstances. God revealed to me that by knowing Him through every high and every low, I could find peace and experience true freedom through His grace. For His Word to transform me, it had to come alive within me. Only then could I share my story and fulfill His mission. Spiritual growth demanded complete surrender; it was not about applying His truth 85% of the time but fully embracing it in every moment and circumstance.

It is your faith that is going to make you well so that you can live in peace. He must be first above your family, your career, your finances, your health. He comes first. Always. "All Scripture is God-breathed and is useful for teaching, rebuking, correcting and training in righteousness, so that the servant of God may be thoroughly equipped for every good work" (2 Timothy 3:16-17). You have to relinquish all control if you want to move forward. Lay it all at the feet of Jesus: the anger, the fear, the weakness, the frailness, the woundedness. King David cried out to the Lord in all of his brokenness in Psalm 51:1-19 after he had committed adultery with Bathsheba.

Have mercy on me, O God, according to your unfailing love; according to your great compassion blot out my transgressions. Wash away all my iniquity and cleanse me from my sin. For

I know my transgressions, and my sin is always before me. Against you, you only, have I sinned and done what is evil in your sight; so you are right in your verdict and justified when you judge. Surely I was sinful at birth, sinful from the time my mother conceived me. Yet you desired faithfulness even in the womb; you taught me wisdom in that secret place. Cleanse me with hyssop, and I will be clean; wash me, and I will be whiter than snow. Let me hear joy and gladness; let the bones you have crushed rejoice. Hide your face from my sins and blot out all my iniquity. Create in me a pure heart, O God, and renew a steadfast spirit within me. Do not cast me from your presence or take your Holy Spirit from me. Restore to me the joy of your salvation and grant me a willing spirit, to sustain me. Then I will teach transgressors your ways, so the sinners will turn back to you. Deliver me from the guilt of bloodshed, O God, you who are God my Savior, and my tongue will sing of your righteousness. Open my lips, Lord, and my mouth will declare your praise. You do not delight in sacrifice, or I would bring it; you do not take pleasure in burnt offerings. My sacrifice, O God, is a broken spirit; a broken and contrite heart you, God, will not despise. May it please you to prosper Zion, to build up the walls of Jerusalem. Then you will delight in the sacrifices of the righteous, in burnt offerings offered whole; then bulls will be offered on your altar.

Over the past two decades, it was only by the hand of God and the people in my life who loved me that I was still even here. It was His providence that led me to where I am today. I was not supposed to remain silent any longer. Yes, I was terrified to take the next step. I knew this was a transition, and a new season awaited. I felt the hand of God saying, *it is time*. I no longer felt the sting of death knocking at my door. It became crystal clear that God wanted me to use all my gut-wrenching, heart-breaking seasons and what I had learned all for His glory. Within every season, He was teaching me how to equip myself and suit up for the battle. I know the pain and agony of the years this sometimes takes; I understand how difficult it is to hang on in those moments. You, my friend, sister, or brother in Christ, are never alone.

One of the last songs I wrote and recorded was *Hang On*. While filming the video in an alley in downtown Winston-Salem, NC, a group of gentlemen were walking by and asking what we were doing. This particular group came to this area every Saturday to meet for breakfast and witness to those in the streets. They asked if they could pray over this video and this song. We stood in a circle in the alley that Saturday morning, and they asked God to use this song to help anyone feeling hopeless and who needed to hear these words. It is a moment in time I will forever cherish.

Hang On

You hurt too much
The pain deep within
All you feel is numb
Hang on
Hang on

Thorns in your side
Drops of tears, you cry
It's so hard to see
Hang on
Hang on

He can hear you when
Calling out His name
He is with you when
Standing in the flames

Draw near

He will draw near you, too, and

Listen

He believes in you

Hold on

His arms are open wide

Draw near

God is on your side

Silence and shame

Only He can understand

His love remains

Hang on

Hang on

He is your friend

You are not alone

With Him, you are strong

Hang on

Hang on

He can hear you when

Calling out His name

He is with you when

Standing in the flames

Draw near

He will draw near you, too, and

Listen

He believes in you

Hold on

His arms are open wide

Draw near

God is on your side

He'll give you peace

Strength, joy again

He'll show you love, truth

Abide in Him

Don't give up now

You'll make it through

Don't give up now

He loves you

He loves you

So much

Draw near

He will draw near you, too, and

Listen

He believes in you

Hold on

His arms are open wide

Draw near

God is on your side

He's on your side

He's on your side

Hold on

Hang on

Draw near[46]

The apostle Paul wrote the following verse: "Whatever you have learned or received or heard from me, or seen in me—put it into practice. And the God of peace will be with you" (Philippians 4:9). He was thanking the Philippians for their generosity in supporting his ministry. He assured them that God would meet their needs as they had met his needs. In times when we are lacking in the belief department, this verse serves as a reminder of His faithfulness and his goodness. We must rely on him and stop letting our concerns eat us alive. I knew the only way to keep moving forward was to seek discernment and wisdom. To live my life in obedience to what the Word of God says.

When conviction is pulling at your heartstrings, press in harder. It is difficult to pray and praise when living in the dark. David was an example of this. In Psalm 34:1-3, he pens, "I will extol the Lord at all times; his praise will always be on my lips. I will glory in the Lord; let the afflicted hear and rejoice. Glorify the Lord with me; let us exalt his name together." We are to shout the name of the Lord! Your walls come down when you shout in praise! It is in the darkness that you are Satan's toy. You are not hopeless; you are not useless. God will give back those years the locusts have eaten in His perfect timing. His way will always win. When we can keep our eyes fixed on the power of the cross, we get to receive the gift of the Holy Spirit working within us and through us all for the glory of God! It is a gift that only God Almighty provides. When the Holy Spirit is speaking through you, people are listening. I was terrified, yet I knew I had to take this step to break free fully. I trusted that God would grant me the boldness and courage I needed—I was all in. Completely immersed. There was no turning back.

---

46 McCutcheon, Jesslyn. "'Hang On." *TuneCore*, 24 Feb. 2023, www.youtube.com/watch?v=xw1e7EZ14ag.

We see countless examples of God equipping the called through the Bible. Moses struggled with God because he felt he was not equipped nor had the tools to do the work God called him to do. God showed him anyway. In Abraham's old age, God placed a call on his life. God did the miraculous and equipped him for it. God desired Abraham to become a source of blessing to the whole world. "I will make you into a great nation; and I will bless you; I will make your name great; and you will be a blessing. I will bless those who bless you, and whoever curses you I will curse; and all peoples on earth will be blessed through you." (Genesis 12:2-3). David had no fundamental skills to be king. God called a sheep header out of his pasture and into the king's palace anyway. King David had a heart for God. Jesus faithfully followed God's call until He was called back to His Father's side to sit at His right hand. Peter had a big mouth and struggled with his faith. God equipped him as he boldly declared the name of Jesus at Pentecost.

If God calls you, you will know and learn to take the exact steps He wants you to take. He doesn't call the qualified, He qualifies those called. I realized that the result did not turn out positive whenever I tried to force or do things on my timeline. If you rush it, you will ruin it. We need the three P's: pause, pray, and be patient. When I listen to what God is telling me, it flows like a river. Beautifully and seamlessly. I was deeply convinced I was being called to serve others with my story. I prayed for God to open the doors he wanted me to walk through and close the doors that needed to be closed. I had an inner peace I had never experienced before. I knew my calling would not be an easy road, but I now had the assurance that I was on the right track. You will learn:

- To hear only HIs voice and leave the world's noise in the background.
- To put Him first among all others and understand His way, not your way.
- To learn that having this opportunity to serve Him will be the most significant gift of your life.

You will finally see that after all you have done, we have a God who loves us despite what our past may bring. I was ready to give and serve the purpose He had created for my life from the beginning. Even though I do live with bipolar disorder, there was freedom in knowing God spoke above any medication or resource that I could take or understand. I was prepared to share that with others.

My story is a story of redemption. It is a story about a God who extended His loving grace and mercy when I was not worthy. My life used to be full of agony. I lived under the radar, in hiding, for two decades! For all the times I thought God went silent, He was there. He was never still.

God will use your adversity to accomplish what He wants you to do for His glory. Sometimes, the goal is not to get rid of the suffering but to endure the suffering well. He is building you and training you, working to develop your character. He is the God who can take tragedy and turn it into something you could never possibly imagine. Something beautiful.

My past needed to stay in the past—it was time to stop looking back. Do you remember what happened to Lot's wife when she looked back at the burning city of Sodom and Gomorrah? The angels told Lot (the nephew of Abraham) and his family to flee from the wicked city. It would be destroyed by God because of the city's wickedness. The angels told them not to look back as they fled the city. Lot's wife had to look. Instantly, she turned into a pillar of salt.

My weakness became my strength and the theme song of my life. Living with bipolar disorder was my weapon to help someone else. He was building the Christ-like character in me that I desperately needed. Every trial was a building block to grow and transform my faith in Him. The time had come when I had to stop running from all the guilt, the shame, and the biggest giant in my life. He forgave me; it was time I forgave myself.

I think about my situation, and then I consider the overwhelming stress that Jesus faced when He was arrested, then tortured, and executed. What unimaginable pain that was for Him. Even though it is challenging to live with a serious mental illness, what I live with is nothing compared to the weight Jesus carried for me and you. Sarah Young, the author of the book, *Jesus Calling*, states in one of her devotionals, "Hope is like a golden cord connecting you to heaven. The more you cling to this cord, the more Jesus bears the weight of our burdens; thus you are lightened. That heaviness is not of His Kingdom, but by clinging to hope His rays of light will reach through the darkness."[47]

We are created for community and fellowship with one another. An opportunity came, and I asked to give my testimony at our Ladies' Prayer Group, which meets once at the beginning of every month at my home church, First Baptist King. I was ready to take the plunge and share what my family and I primarily kept to ourselves for many years. I could not stay silent any longer—I was no longer afraid. The blood of Jesus Christ protected me and He was not done with me yet. I did not want to run the race of fear any longer. I tried to walk by faith and with the confidence that I was not a failure. I was never alone. I was ready to take hold of every thought. I knew that God had an assignment just for me. Proverbs 24:16 declares: "For though the righteous fall seven times, they rise again about the wicked stumble when calamity strikes." Where the Spirit of the Lord is, there is freedom. The *I Am* statements in the Gospel of John are profound and rich in wisdom and their meaning. Let us look at these statements together and their meanings:

- **"I am the bread of life."**

  Jesus offers spiritual nourishment for our souls. Just as bread feeds our human flesh, he sustains spiritual life for those who believe and trust in Him (John 6:35).

---

47   Sarah Young, *Jesus Calling: Enjoying Peace in His Presence*, Thomas Nelson, 2004, p.11.

- **"I am the light of the world."**

  When you follow Jesus, you do not have to live in a dungeon of darkness. He provides the hope to keep you going and a way out (John 8:12).

- **"I am the gate of the sheep."**

  Jesus is the Lamb of God and the gateway of our salvation. Through Him, believers find refuge under His watchful eye and protection (John 10:7).

- **"I am the Good Shepherd."**

  Jesus guides and cares for His followers, makes sacrifices, and He laid His life down for His followers (John 10:11).

- **"I am the resurrection and the life."**

  You must believe that even though life here on earth is not forever, there is eternal life for whoever lives by believing. He has the authority to defeat death just like He did for all of us on the cross at Calvary (John 11:25).

- **"I am the way, the truth, and the life."**

  The only reconciliation with God is through Him (John 14:6).

- **"I am the true vine."**

  We are called to connect to Him, like branches on a vine. In doing so, we can bear spiritual fruit (John 15:1).

- **"Before Abraham was born, I Am."**

  Jesus existed before Abraham. He identified with God before Abraham was even in the picture. He identified Himself with eternal nature (John 8:58).

At some point, you have to shake off your chains of death and let the Good Shepherd lead. Come trembling, falling at his feet. Even if you are living with a chronic mental health condition, God has the power to bring you back to life! You have to tell yourself that no amount of pain will keep you from following Christ. You may get knocked down repeatedly, but with Christ, you will never be defeated. Do not suppress the Holy Spirit.

The cross is a gift—I owe my life to Him. It was time that I stopped living in my past and knew that the cross was the only way I was ever going to reach freedom. God does not want bits and pieces of you. God wants all of you. My medication, the doctors, therapy, ECT treatments, and hospitalizations all played active roles in helping me and are all critical treatment options if necessary. However, none of those treatments provided me with the ultimate freedom of knowing Christ like I do now. I knew that for all the madness to stop, if I was ever going to win the fight, I had to stop running, hiding from God, myself, and the world. I had to let others know that I am not ashamed of who I am or living with the giant of a mental illness. If truth be told, it is because of my mental illness that I know God like I do today. He uses our weakness, the least of these, to accomplish things for His glory.

Each day, we can choose compassion and empathy toward others. Being a Christian means continuously growing to reflect His love in our actions and attitudes, even when it is difficult. The way we treat others reflects our faith, and each choice we make has the power to shine His light in a hurting world.

In Luke 10:25-35, an expert in the Jewish law asks Jesus this question: "Teacher, what must I do to inherit eternal life?" Jesus responds with a question: "What is written in the law?" The lawyer answered, "Love the Lord your God with all your heart, mind, and soul, and that we should love our neighbor as yourself." Jesus replied that he was correct in his answer. The lawyer then asks the question, "Who is my neighbor?" Jesus begins to share a story about love that knows no boundaries. A man was traveling from Jerusalem to Jericho when he was attacked, stripped of his clothes, beaten, and left half-dead on the side of the road by robbers. The first person to see the man was a priest who happened to be going down the same route. What did he do? When he saw the man, he passed by and walked on the other side.

Next, a Levite (or a temple assistant) also traveled that same road, saw the man, and he, too, passed by on the other side. Finally, a third man, a Samaritan, traveled the same road where he came to where the man was. When he saw him, he had compassion on the man, went to his need, bandaged his wounds by pouring oil and wine on them, and then placed the man on his donkey where he took him to an inn to care for him. He gave the innkeeper two denarii (two days' wages) the following day and said, "Take care of him. When I return, I will reimburse you for any extra expense." He loved his neighbor. He treated another in the same way he would like to be treated—with mercy and kindness regardless of age, race, or religion. He did not just check to see if he was alright; he took action. What the Samaritan shows is that love is demonstrated through taking action. Sometimes, all a person needs is to be loved by someone else to see them through.

It took me a very long time to accept my condition and what I have had to deal with throughout the years. I resigned from jobs as the depression and mania took hold, friendships strained, bridges burned, and I missed out on important life events and faced financial struggles. I had to forgive myself. I was not my illness; you are not your illness. Your illness does not define who you are and what you are capable of as a person. My identity is not that I live with bipolar disorder. My identity and how I manage to stay in recovery while living with bipolar disorder is by knowing and remembering that Jesus Christ is the source of our life. True repentance is rooted in a sincere, biblical understanding of our identity. I am not a failure because of my life's twists and turns. Any shame, heartache, and hurt all had to be buried for me to walk forward. How did David win the fight with Goliath? Knowing that his identity and trust were in the only One who could give him the courage, the strength, and the ability to TAKE GOLIATH DOWN.

There is nothing wrong with living with a mental health condition. Even though I will still have bad days, which are inevitable when living with bipolar disorder, the darkness will not overtake me when those days come. The days when mania comes, I will be a soldier, keep fighting, and never forget who He says I am, even when the world wants me to believe otherwise. Death has no power over me anymore. Trusting in His amazing grace can turn a life around. I am taking back what the enemy has stolen from me for many years. I am taking it all back! When you walk with God, there is a way out. The giants of life we face do not have to have the last word. Jesus was concerned with culture and intensely focused on the human heart–loving people as you are and loving me just as I am.

In 1835, Charlotte Elliott of Brighton, England, wrote the below lyrics. Charlotte and I had something in common. We both became bitter and resentful over the years, living with health issues that hardened our hearts. We both could not fully understand why God would let this go on for many years. You cannot cling to your anger. You will only get better when you decide to cling to the cross. What was my cure, then? My faith and a transformation of the heart.

Just As I Am

Just as I am, without one plea
But that Thy blood was shed for me,
And that Thou bidst me come to Thee,
O Lamb of God, I come, I come.

Just as I am, and waiting not
To rid my soul of one dark blot,
To Thee whose blood can cleanse each spot,
O Lamb of God, I come, I come.

Just as I am, through tossed about
With many a conflict, many a doubt,
Fightings within and fears without,
O Lamb of God, I come, I come.

Just as I am, poor, wretched blind,
Sight, riches, healing of the mind,
Yea, all I need in Thee to find,
O Lamb of God, I come, I come.

Just as I am, Thou wilt receive,
With welcome, pardon, cleanse, relieve;
Because Thy promise I believe,
O Lamb of God, I come, I come![48]

---

48 Elliott, Charlotte. *Just As I Am*, 1835.

CHAPTER 12

SINGING JAILBIRD

"Sing to the Lord a new song; sing to the Lord, all the earth. Sing to the Lord, praise his name, proclaim his salvation day after day.
—Psalm 96:1-2

When words fail me, I sing—He is worthy of our praise! Worship through song brings me back to the core of my identity in Jesus Christ, grounding me in truth. Singing lets me pour out my heart, releasing fears, worries, and negativity. In the darkest nights, sometimes singing is my only lifeline; even when storms rage, His words flow like fire, reviving me. His gentle whisper reveals truth over lies, reminding me that my soul needs a friend, and He sees me and gets me how I am. When our worship is Spirit-led, it becomes more than singing—it becomes a connection that speaks to the body, mind, and soul.

Music communicates emotion. When music is nothing but groans and pain, He is listening. He sees you sitting under the fig tree, whether you realize this or not. When the music is full of joy, He is listening. When your heart is captivated by worship, you are left speechless.

Jesus sang the melody meant to echo through our lives each day. In His moment of abandonment, as He hung on the cross, He cried out, "My God, my God, why have you forsaken me?..." (Psalm 22:1). He sang that song as a sacrifice for our sins to save our souls, to offer us refuge, and to help us rise from our brokenness and rubble.

Living with bipolar disorder and depression can hover like a dark storm cloud, striking unexpectedly—triggered by circumstances, stress, or how well you are taking care of yourself. One Sunday, Jason took the girls to church while I stayed home, feeling the heavy weight of depression settling over me again. We both knew this was not going to be a good day. I felt completely numb, wrestling with thoughts of my existence and wondering how I could continue like this—riding an emotional roller coaster that never ends. With bipolar disorder, there is no option to stop the ride and step off; you are forced to hold on, even on the days when you are barely hanging on by a thread.

The darkness wrapped me in a blanket of despair. Moments like these require something powerful to break the chains and bring your freedom back. That morning, I had not planned to watch the service online; I only wanted to sleep, hoping to escape the noise swirling in my head. At this depth of depression, even small actions feel unbearably heavy—turning over in bed, reaching for the remote, or trying to turn on the TV feels like a workout, draining every ounce of energy. But instead of trying to drown out the noise in my head with sleep, I watched the service, hoping to silence the relentless voices telling me I could not keep going on. The sermon titled: *From Trashed to Treasured*, was pivotal—it helped me find solid ground again.

Transformation begins when we hear His Word but actively put it into practice, embracing His shield of protection. Applying His truth to your life is essential. In moments of darkness, He must be your flashlight of hope. Pain can cloud your vision and deafen your heart, making it hard to see or hear Him. Even as Christians, we can become spiritually blind, but God has His ways of breaking through. Sometimes, it takes hitting a wall to realize you are on a path toward destruction. To fully grasp His promises, your heart and mind must be fully invested in your relationship with Jesus. Without faith, His plans and purposes remain incomplete in your understanding. That day, after hearing His message, I felt something shift. I rose from bed, grabbed my journal, found a pen, and went to my prayer closet. A sacred space where God and I had shared some of our most intimate conversations. Behind those closed doors, through tears, struggle, hurt, pain, and brokenness, I began to write. It was at that moment that these lyrics poured out from my heart. As He spoke, the words came flowing like a river:

You worry
Some say a little way too much
Excuse me for this
Who are you to judge
There is only so much
You can do in times like these
But something happens
When I get on my knees

I roar louder
When the fear creeps inside
I pray harder
I watch the doubt start to subside
I think Jesus
When the dark clouds roll on through
I roar louder
Pray harder
Let mercy rescue you

You are brave
So much stronger than you think
I stand amazed
When I fly under His wings
I may not know

The course I am gonna go
But I will follow
He will lead me on this road, this road

I roar louder
When the fear creeps inside
I pray harder
I watch the doubt start to subside
I think Jesus
When the dark clouds roll on through
I roar louder
Pray harder
Let mercy rescue you

Just have faith
And you won't ever be
Destroyed
Or washed into some raging sea
I don't want to be just a fan
I want to have faith
And now I am in your hands

I roar louder
When the fear creeps inside
I pray harder
I watch the doubt start to subside
I think Jesus
When the dark clouds roll on through

I roar louder

Pray harder

Let mercy rescue you

I roar louder

Pray harder

Let mercy rescue you

Let mercy rescue you

When doubts arise, reflect on His faithfulness in your past troubles. Time and time again, He has pulled me from the fire. Worship always has a way of leading me back into the presence of God, reminding me of the times He has already uprooted me. You must be confident that He uprooted before and He will do it again. In life, *Goliaths* come in many different forms—a job situation, your finances, struggle with your marriage, unhappy relationships. When in battle, victory is achieved by knowing Jesus, regardless of how big your struggle may be. When David was about to face the 9'9" Goliath, He believed that victory and triumph were certain because He came in the name of the Lord. Your battles may be big, but they pale compared to Jesus's vastness and the cross's power. Cling to the Spirit of the Lord with all your strength, might, and soul. When your mind is filled with the goodness of God, His Spirit helps restore your mind to a place of clarity and truth. Let the songs in your heart flow out as an offering, a reminder of His sustaining presence.

The book of Psalms is a collection of 150 poetic hymns in the Bible's Old Testament. It is a beautiful book organized into five smaller books, each one closing with the doxology, which means the study of praise. This book of the Bible inspired our daughter's name, Selah. The name appears 71 times in the Book of Psalms—as a beautiful reminder to pause and reflect on His Word, character, and works. I often turn to the book of Psalms when I need to quiet my mind in worship, engage in personal devotion, or pour my heart out in prayer. During my darkest moments of depression, the Psalms became my anchor, my guide, and my sustenance, offering words to express my laments before the Lord while also reminding me of His enduring presence and faithfulness.

> Hear my prayer, Lord;
>
> let my cry for help come to you.
>
> Do not hide your face from me
>
> when I am in distress.
>
> Turn your ear to me;
>
> when I call, answer me quickly.
>
> For my days vanish like smoke;
>
> my bones burn like glowing embers.
>
> My heart is blighted and withered like grass;
>
> I forget to eat my food.
>
> In my distress, I groan aloud
>
> and am reduced to skin and bone.
>
> I am like a desert owl,
>
> like an owl among the ruins.
>
> I lie awake; I have become
>
> like a bird alone on a roof.
>
> All day long my enemies taunt me;
>
> those who rail against me use my name as a curse.
>
> For I eat ashes as my food
>
> and mingle my drink with tears
>
> because of your great wrath,
>
> for you have taken me up and
>
> thrown me aside.

My days are like the evening shadow;

I wither away like the grass (Psalm 102:1-11).

The book of Psalms is not the only book in the Bible with praise songs. Both the New and Old Testaments incorporate songs of praise. One song we have heard and may be familiar with is *Gloria in Excelsis Deo,* the song of the angels in Luke 2:14: "Glory to God in the highest heaven and on earth peace to those on whom his favor rests."

Job is one of the oldest books in the Bible. He was a wealthy farmer from a place called Uz. God grants the devil permission to attack Job and his possessions, family, and health. Satan wipes out thousands of camels, oxen, donkeys, sheep, and his ten children. All of his children at once! After his possessions and children had been taken, "At this, Job got up, tore his robe and, shaved his head. Then he fell to the ground in **worship** and said: 'Naked I came from my mother's womb, and naked I will depart. The Lord gave and the Lord has taken away; may the name of the Lord be praised" (Job 1:20-21, emphasis added). Despite all of his suffering, Job does not curse the name of God, but he praises Him. By the end of the book of Job, God restores his possessions, health, and family by giving him ten more children.

Worship is not about our feelings; it is not about the praise team or the Minister of Music on Sundays. Worship belongs to God and not to another. He is the only One who deserves your worship.

"Where is the one who has been born king of the Jews? We saw his star when it rose and have come to **worship** him" (Matthew 2:2, emphasis added).

"Then Herod called the Magi secretly and found out from them the exact time the star had appeared. He sent them to Bethlehem and said, 'Go and search carefully for the child. As soon as you find him, report to me, so that I too may go and **worship** him" (Matthew 2:7-8, emphasis added).

"On coming to the house, they saw the child with his mother Mary, and they bowed down and **worshiped** him. Then they opened their treasures and presented him with gifts of gold, frankincense and myrrh" (Matthew 2:11, emphasis added).

Worship is rooted in your faith. I never broke when I worshipped through every storm I faced, whether it was due to my illness or other circumstances. The exact opposite happened. Worship provides the hope I need, especially when I cannot hold on any longer. When suffering drags on, and the battle feels too overwhelming, your heart is shattered, and you are filled with unanswered questions, you have nothing left to give—worship remains. The invitation is always open and waiting for us to arrive. Even when your world is shaking and the darkness seems to close in, worship will keep you grounded in the light, preventing you from being swallowed up whole by the devil of despair. Every time, God delivered me and rescued me, when I cried during my worship. "Praise the Lord. How good is it to sing praises to our God, how pleasant and fitting to praise him!" (Psalm 147:1).

Genuine worship comes when you learn how to bow the knee. You know how to treat people how they need to be treated after you worship, you cannot have genuine worship when you live a double life. You worship one way but treat people another. Only you know what needs to be fixed on the inside. Freedom can be found when you give your whole heart to Christ. True worship is truth that can transcend time and space. Worshipping is a melody of redemption. As you learn to submit everything within you to the king of your heart, your character starts to change—you change. People begin to notice the change in you, and this is where you can help build God's church. Scripture tells us in John 4:23-24, "Yet a time is coming and has now come when the true worshipers will worship the Father in the Spirit and in truth, for they are the kind of worshipers the Father seeks. God is spirit, and his worshipers must worship in the Spirit and truth." This was when Jesus spoke with the woman at the well. She learned that the only one able to quench her thirst was the living water only God can provide. Are you weary from getting thirsty? Do you long to drink from the eternal well that will quench your thirst forever? I strive to be this kind of worshiper—one who worships through trials, lives a life of obedience, prioritizes time with God, and worships with humility and gratitude.

The Bible tells us we can sing, clap, bow the knee, raise our hands in praise; we can even dance in church. You can go to church and do all these things. You can worship your way out of your circumstances. When you seek the Kingdom of God, He will give you treasures. Take your pain, sorrow, despair, ruins, killed dreams and plans and worship. We will never know or can comprehend what God is doing behind the scenes. God knows things that you do not know. The conversations people have behind your back, those plotting evil against you, those speaking negatively about you—can renew your mind and help you overcome your weaknesses and barriers. *War-ship* can break your prison chains. Acts 16:25-26 tells us when the prison chains broke for Paul and Silas through their *war-ship*. They both were imprisoned in Philippi after being falsely accused by the owners of a slave girl whom Paul freed from a spirit of divination:

"About midnight Paul and Silas were praying and singing hymns to God, and the other prisoners were listening to them. Suddenly there was such a violent earthquake that the foundations of the prison were shaken. At once all the prison doors flew open, and everyone's chains came loose" (Acts 16:25-26).

What kind of love heals, lifts, and brings you back to life? Only this kind of love comes from Christ. Despite the amount of suffering that may come, I have made worship a lifestyle. In return, it has transformed me into a new creation.

In the Summer of 2020, I had my second cervical fusion neck surgery due to a second rupture performed on the C-6/C-7 level. My anxiety was high. I was crying and scared. On this particular morning, transport was on their way to take me down for surgery. Jason and my nurse huddled with me around my bed. They were both trying to console me and calm me down. What started as crying turned into panic.

Earthquakes are unusual in North Carolina, but they can happen. In August 2020, a 5.1 magnitude earthquake centered near Sparta, NC. This earthquake caused significant damage and created the first seismic faulting surface rupture documented in the Eastern United States. It was the second-strongest earthquake to strike the East Coast since the 2011 Virginia earthquake. It was the strongest earthquake recorded in North Carolina in 104 years. A state of emergency was issued for North Carolina, and $24 million in relief funds were issued for the damage it has caused.

For those brief moments, Jason, the nurse, and I experienced the earthquake together. The hospital floor beneath us trembled, and everything fell silent. We exchanged startled glances, asking, *"Did you feel that?"* The nurse, now visibly shaken, quickly sat down on my bed. Her panic is setting in. In that instant, my problem seemed incredibly small in comparison. We cannot even fathom the vastness of God and His works. When I am without God, I shake. When I am with God, nothing can shake me. The song below was written in my hospital bed during my recovery that day. *What Kind of Love Is This?* That He would love such a wretch as me? This was my cry of *war-ship*.

What Kind Of Love Is This

Let it pour down

Let it rain

Test this broken heart of mine

Let the earthquake

Let it shake

Open up these tear-stained eyes

Let the pain burn

Let it burn

I know you're right here by my side

Let the page turn
Let it turn
Close this chapter in my life

What Kind Of Love Is This
To come back every time
With open arms for me
To bind these wounds of mine
What kind of love is this
One would lay down His own life
What kind of love is this
What kind of love is this

Peace be still now
Peace be still
Calm my sea of Galilee

Do not fear
Don't wither down
'Cause His mercy covers me

You will rise you'll stand again
You're gonna live to testify
Because of Him
Because of Christ
There is everlasting life

What kind of love is this
To come back every time

With open arms for me
To bind these wounds of mine
What kind of love is this
One would lay down his own life
What kind of love is this
What kind of love is this

Let the darkness turn to light
Brighter than noonday
Let the hope in me come alive
I will not be afraid

Let the darkness turn to light
Brighter than noonday
Let the hope in me come alive
I will not be afraid
I will not be afraid
I will not be afraid
I will not be afraid

What kind of love is this
To come every time
With open arms for me
To bind these wounds of mine
What kind of love is this
One would lay down His own life
What kind of love is this
What kind of love is this

What kind of love is this

What kind of love is this

What kind of love is this[49]

This chapter and song are lovingly dedicated to my dear friend, Benny Stoltz. I had the privilege and honor of recording this piece in his studio in Winston-Salem, NC. Benny had a deep love for the Lord. We shared a passion for worshiping and creating music–a bond I will forever hold close to my heart. When Benny passed away, it was a privilege to sing *What Kind Of Love Is This* at his funeral—a moment that reflected his unwavering faith. His life brings to mind the words of David: "I keep my eyes always on the Lord, with him at my right hand, I will not be shaken" (Psalm 16:8).

---

49 McCutcheon, Jesslyn. *What Kind of Love Is This.* TuneCore, 24 Feb. 2023. YouTube, https://youtu.be/5sAJ1iBI19U.

CHAPTER 13

IT IS WELL WITH MY SOUL

"I will not die but live, and will proclaim what the Lord has done."
—Psalm 118:17

The legacy of brokenness began in the very beginning when Adam and Eve disobeyed God in the Garden of Eden. Since that moment, humanity has lived in a state of destruction. Today, vulnerability is evident everywhere—fractured lives and broken hearts, desperate for healing. Our pain creates separation between us and the Father, yet there is hope. In 1 Corinthians 15:45-46, Paul reminds us: "The first man Adam became a living being; the last Adam, a life-giving spirit. The spiritual did not come first, but the natural, and after that the spiritual." Jesus came to save us from our sins, heal our pain, and deliver us from suffering.

Living with bipolar disorder brought deep-seated pain. I did not want to have to accept or own up to living with a brain-based illness. My attitude and my sense of perspective had to come with accepting the illness. It did not seem fair, and life did not make sense. Life with bipolar disorder, many times, seemed too hard just to be alive. I would never be able to see the whole picture and my life's purpose until I learned that Jesus Christ was the only way. "For my thoughts are not your thoughts, neither are your ways my ways," declares the Lord. (Isaiah 55:8).

There are some questions we will never know the answers to. Why? Because we cannot see the entire picture. We are not God. We do not always understand what is good or bad, nor do we possess the authority to judge. Life is uncertain, but one thing remains steadfast:

God is good. Those words are simple yet powerful. He is perfect and holy. God does not change (Malachi 3:6). When we do not understand, we can trust His goodness. Comfort comes from knowing we do not need all the answers, for His ways are righteous, honorable, correct, and trustworthy. In times of pain and suffering—do not push Him away. Instead, it says in James 4:8, "Come near to God and he will come near to you…" These are the moments when we need Him most. Where we fail short, God prevails. Stop fighting a battle that He won over 2,000 years ago. Out illness, shame, failures, or regrets must be laid at the feet of Jesus. Every scar serves a purpose–the stains life brings can be wiped clean. Through all the wreckage, remember this: He is right there, waiting to carry you home.

Sometimes, living with a mental illness, you feel like there is nowhere to turn. You do not feel understood or that anyone is going to understand. You keep your intrusive thoughts to yourself and deal with the pain of suffering in silence. We long for people to want to learn and accept that the human being is both physical and mental. We long to not be cast aside and to not feel the rejection by others that constantly flows like a river. We yearn not to feel all alone. Here is the best news: You are never alone. Millions of people live with bipolar disorder, and some want to see you regain control of your life. He is more than capable of moving mountains and breaking chains. Hope is never lost because there are resources, good mental health professionals, and people who do understand. More importantly, there is still an empty grave! You have the authority to declare truth in your life. Are you ready to follow in His footsteps even through all the pain? The world and the flesh will never provide you the security only God can. Your pain does have a cure, and His name is Jesus, the Savior of the World.

We live in a frightening time where even watching the news can leave us feeling sick and overwhelmed. Yet Jesus came to save the broken—people like you and me—and to bring peace to our hearts. He has overcome the world. The future often feels shrouded in darkness and unanswerable questions. However, we can take comfort in knowing God is always at work. It is not easy to hear that we should rejoice in tribulation—how do we do this? We shift our focus from the problem to the Provider by gaining a new perspective. We are called to take heart, hold onto hope, and take up our cross to follow Him. Even when the weight feels unbearable, keep the faith and know you are not forsaken. Stay the course. In the depths of depression and mania and recovery, we look to Him. Through trials, we gain strength and perseverance. You must believe even when the season in your life is challenging. He will uphold you with His righteous right hand (Isaiah 41:10). He is God, and we are not.

Have you discovered the passion you can feel in your bones from finding the freedom in Jesus Christ? Do you know you are fully loved and accepted just as you are? This freedom does not mean that we are no longer going to struggle with our mental illness. This freedom brings a new kind of strength and the courage to face the challenges that come with living with bipolar disorder. You are no longer a prisoner to the opinion of others or bad choices and mistakes you have made in the past. Instead, your life becomes anchored in His truth that God's love is constant, His mercy is unending, and His plans for you are for the good. "Then you will know the truth, and the truth will set you free" (John 8:32).

I did not genuinely understand what it meant to be *made for more*. I did not know how to let go of my past and move forward without looking back. I had to return to being a praying woman to rediscover my true inheritance and identity in Christ. Today, I am firmly rooted and built up in Him. I have been rescued from Satan's domain and transferred into the arms of Jesus. God gives me a spirit of power, love, and self-discipline. I have been bought with a price and belong to God. I am a daughter of the highest King, the Anointed One, assured that all things work together for good (Romans 8:28). This verse is a beautiful reminder of His faithfulness and ability to bring meaning out of even the most demanding circumstances. Life can be challenging, complicated, formidable, and complex. We can trust that His purpose for our lives will unfold perfectly.

Bipolar disorder is a chronic illness that will continue to impact my life and require ongoing management. There is no cure. Those of us living with bipolar disorder know that this journey is for life. However, when you genuinely understand the thorn in your side for what it is, there is no greater love. God uses our struggles—the thorns and thistles of our lives as reminders that His strength is made perfect in our weaknesses. In Paul's letter to the Corinthians, he reflects on his challenges:

> "To keep me from becoming conceited, I was given a thorn in my flesh, a messenger of Satan, to torment me. Three times I pleaded with the Lord to take it away from me. But he said to me, 'My grace is sufficient for you, for my power is made perfect in weakness.' Therefore I will boast all the more gladly about my weaknesses, so that Christ's power may rest on me. That is why, for Christ's sake, I delight in weaknesses, in insults, in hardships, in persecutions, in difficulties. For when I am weak, then I am strong" (2 Corinthians 12:7-10).

Through my journey, as difficult as it has been to live with bipolar I disorder, I have come to realize I needed this *thorn*. In my weakest moments, my *thorn* always points me back to the cross when I fall short. I know some of you reading this may wonder how I could ever be thankful for living with such a challenging illness. The answer is simple: the *thorn* inspired the writing of this book. I would not know Him like I do today without the *thorn*. His unconditional love has rescued me from the pit more than I can count. He has given me new eyes to see that I cannot live with bipolar disorder without Him. There are no words to fully express my complete gratitude for His love and grace. He leaves me breathtakingly speechless.

When you root your identity in Christ, the confidence provided by the Holy Spirit empowers you to accomplish things you once believed impossible. I can say with certainty that I would not have the courage to be this vulnerable—sharing my story with you—if I did not trust my journey was sealed in His hands. How do we move from the depths of darkness to the brilliance of His light? The answer lies in discovering a balance that embraces seeking help, finding hope, and pursuing healing. Let us explore some essential steps to illuminate the path out of the darkness and into His light.

- **Your spiritual maturity and hope:**

  "But those who hope in the Lord shall renew their strength. They will soar on wings like eagles; they will run and not grow weary, they will walk and not be faint" (Isaiah 40:31).

  "Your word is a lamp unto my feet, a light on my path" (Psalm 119:105).

  Prayer and meditation.

- **Seek help:**

  Find a mental health professional who can offer a proper diagnosis. If you are not connecting with that provider, find someone you can connect with. Do not be ashamed to seek therapy such as CBT (cognitive behavioral therapy) and family-focused therapy. Take notes of all side effects from any medications that you are trying. Often, there were times I could not remember all the side effects if I had not written them down by the time the appointment came. Regular appointments and honest communication with a healthcare provider are crucial in maintaining your overall mental health.

- **Community:**

  Surround yourself with the people who want to be there for you. The people that accept you for the exact person that you are. If this is not your family or friends, find a support group and meet people who understand—this can make a huge difference. Living in isolation and fear will disable you. It is just not healthy. The power of collective action with others makes all the difference!

- **Your Identity:**

  As you go through your journey, always remember that you are not your illness. Your identity is not bipolar. You live with bipolar disorder. You are a person first. You have a name, hopes, and dreams, and you have your unique skills. You are not faceless. Your illness does not limit you from achieving your goals. You can move towards the light in the healing process. The only person to decide your identity is Jesus—put on Christ and fight!

- **Finding Your Purpose:**

  Many people who live with bipolar disorder find hope in sharing their stories with others. Finding that your story and journey might be part of a greater purpose can be transformative. He uses the misfits, the underestimated, and those considered unworthy by society because His strength is made perfect in weakness. Remember, God does not waste wounds. He knows what being alone, rejected, and misunderstood feels like. He has provided a place for us to call home.

My journey has had many challenges—rocky, rough, and unpaved. That is life. I am in awe of the incredible, humbling love my Father has shown me. Abba, the Creator of the heavens and the earth, loves me—broken and imperfect as I am. At times, I am a hot mess. The weight of heaviness no longer holds power over me. I have discovered a purpose far higher than myself and found my identity in Christ. He is my strength, shield, and hope—a song I will carry forever.

I am reminded of David, who faced what seemed impossible: slaying a giant. To many, it looked hopeless. But with the favor of God in his heart, David overcame the 9'9" giant who mocked David, ridiculed him, and laughed at him. Goliath, a seasoned warrior armed with powerful weapons, underestimated the strength of faith. Living with bipolar disorder often feels like facing a giant every single day. Few understand the mental and emotional battles that rage within, and even fewer grasp the resilience it takes to endure. Prideful hearts and

His presence do not mix, so do not let others define your worth. Please do not let anyone dismiss your struggles simply because they cannot see them. Mental health conditions are very real and are severe medical conditions. If only people could see the person instead of the illness, the world would be kinder and more compassionate.

When discovering your identity, you may find that it's taking a long time. This book is a collaboration of my life from the past 25 years. When we wait, He reminds us of His perfect timing. His perfect payment was the life of His perfect Son. Say goodbye to the old and hello to being made new in Christ! "Therefore, if anyone is in Christ, the new creation has come: The old has gone, the new is here!" (2 Corinthians 5:17). Here are some biblical examples of why God may make us wait:

- **To build our trust:**

  In the Bible, the Israelites waited 40 years in the wilderness, not only because of their disobedience but also to learn to rely entirely on the Lamb of God (Joshua 5:6).

- **To gain patience:**

  Abraham and Sarah waited 25 years for their promised son, Isaac. During all that time, God tested their faith and taught them patience (Genesis 12 & Genesis 21:5).

- **To wait to see the magnificence of His power–which will be magnified when your breakthrough finally arrives:**

  When Lazarus died, Jesus delayed His friend's resurrection. This waiting declared that Jesus had all authority over life and death (John 11:1-45).

- **To teach us humility:**

  Joseph waited years in slavery and prison before God raised him to a position in Egypt. During this time, Joseph's faith grew, and he could forgive his brothers and reunite with his family (Genesis 37-41).

- **To have a heart that is only for Jesus:**

  Hannah waited and prayed for a son, and through her waiting, she learned that she desired to rely on God. Her son, Samuel, became one of Israel's greatest prophets

  (1 Samuel 1:1-28).

No matter how often the enemy sits at your table, I pray you are taking a seat by the Savior. For those labeled right or wrong or prisoners of past mistakes, there is freedom found in knowing Christ.

I encourage you to be a David and fight your Goliaths. You can do this. You can live a fulfilled life with bipolar disorder. Do not give up. Never give up. No one understands as God does. Let Him in. Lay it all down. Hang on to the hem of His garment for your dear life! "If I just touch his clothes, I will be healed" (Mark 5:28). He loves you through every season. Through every battle cry of despair, every moment you cannot summon the energy to shower, brush your teeth, or eat—through every hospitalization, medication change, panic attack, manic episode, or depressive struggle–through humiliation and the hurtful words spoken by others, He sees you. Someone sees you. Let go of the shame and guilt that seek to control you. With this mindset, the devil cannot touch you. His blood has redeemed you. Even when the waters feel deep, remember that with the favor of God, you will not sink. Step confidently into the water, knowing you will not be overwhelmed or drowned.

God is for you, not against you. Scripture tells us in Numbers 6:24-26:

The Lord bless you

and keep you;

the Lord make his face shine on you

and be gracious to you;

the Lord turn his face toward you

and give you peace.

Face living with a mental illness head-on. Look it straight in the eyes, rather than burying your face in the dirt, believing you do not deserve a good life or it is impossible. It will be one of the fiercest battles you will ever fight, and there will be moments when you want to give up. **Do not listen to the voice. It is a lie! Never stop fighting!** Even if you have one smooth stone to take from your bag, put it in your sling and face the giant!

God places a Goliath in your life to help you discover your inner David. Do not let your Goliath be your death sentence. Struggles can refine our character and strengthen our faith like fire refines gold. Through these challenges, God shapes us into sturdier, more resilient people, preparing us for the purpose He had planned for our lives from the beginning. "For I know the plans that I have for you," declares the Lord. "Plans to prosper you and not to harm you, plans to give you hope and a future. Then you will call on me and come and pray to me, and I will listen to you. You will seek me and find me when you seek me with all your heart." (Jeremiah 29:11-12). Step into the battle with faith, trust, courage, obedience, and praise, knowing that through Him, anything is possible.

Life is unpredictable and can change instantly. True peace flows like a river through a relationship with Christ. The loss that has tried to take you down over all these years cannot compare to what is waiting for all who choose to believe. Christ secured the victory on the cross long ago.

My peace can only be found in the true hero of this story, knowing that Jesus Christ is Lord over my life—the peace that surpasses all understanding. I now can boldly declare: *It is well with my soul.* Now—**go and slay your giant!**

It Is Well With My Soul

When peace like a river attendeth my way

When sorrows like sea billows roll

Whatever my lot, Thou hast taught me to say
It is well, it is well, with my soul

It is well (it is well)
With my soul (with my soul)
It is well, it is well with my soul.

My sin, oh, the bliss of this glorious thought
My sin, not in part but the whole
Is nailed to the cross and I bear it no more
Praise the Lord, praise the Lord, oh, my soul

It is well (it is well)
With my soul (with my soul)
It is well, it is well with my soul

And Lord haste the day
when my faith shall be sight
The clouds be rolled back as a scroll
The trump shall resound
and the Lord shall descend
Even so, it is well with my soul

It is well (it is well)
With my soul (with my soul)

It is well with my soul.[50]

---

50 Spafford, Horatio. *It Is Well With My Soul.* Composed by Philip Bliss, 1873.

A NOTE TO THE READER

Dear friend,

This book was not written by accident—sharing my story had been part of His plan all along.

I once saw myself as a bruised and forgotten child, forced into a life that I would have never chosen for myself–living with bipolar disorder—an illness I once despised, carrying deep bitterness, especially when facing misunderstandings and judgments from others. I feared stepping away from His Will would lead Him to abandon me. But my friend, God does not do such a thing! He saw the potential in my heart to fulfill His Will. He saw me as a lost sheep who wept with a broken soul. Through my journey with this illness, I have discovered my true purpose at the feet of Jesus.

To the reader who is a caretaker:

The role of a caretaker is challenging and can often feel exhausting. It is natural to prioritize your loved one's needs, but this can sometimes lead to neglecting your well-being. Remember, your mental health is just as important as theirs. Take time to rest, seek support, and care for yourself. If you do not take care of yourself, you cannot take care of your loved one effectively. Continuing to educate yourself about bipolar disorder, listen without judgment, encourage a treatment plan, and celebrate small victories are all powerful ways to support your loved one. This journey will be overwhelming at times. There are moments when you will feel unappreciated or unsure of your efforts. Never lose sight that you are a lifeline to the person you love. Hold onto hope, knowing your role makes a difference. The one living with bipolar disorder deeply values you, even if it is not always expressed. The gratitude for all you do is more than words could ever say.

To the reader who is a mental health professional:

Thank you for taking the time to read this book. It is truly humbling to know that someone who makes such a meaningful impact in the mental health field would invest their time in my work and my story. I hope that sharing my journey and lived experience brings greater understanding and sheds light on those who live with bipolar disorder. Your tireless efforts to bring hope, support, and healing to those navigating this condition are deeply appreciated, and I am grateful for all you do.

To the reader who supports mental health through our community, workplace, churches, or support groups:

Thank you for your commitment, empathy, and the difference that you make daily within our communities, workplaces, churches, and support groups. I appreciate your dedication to building bridges of hope and helping to break down the stigma surrounding mental health. I hope that my story can serve as a resource and encouragement for ongoing efforts to advocate for others who live with a mental illness.

To the reader who supported my book, even though it did not apply to you:

Your choice to support this book encourages awareness, breaks down stigma, and fosters conversations with others to let them know they are less alone. For your support, I am grateful. You are making a difference just by supporting this book.

To the reader who lives with bipolar disorder:

I see you, and more importantly, God sees you. He does not desire you to remain in the pit of despair forever. Yes, those of us who live with bipolar disorder will continue to have mania and depression. However, because of my relationship with Him, I know there is always an exit, a way out. While illnesses like bipolar disorder may not have a cure, there is a transformation of the heart that can take place.

All you need is to believe that Jesus died for you and trust that He can rescue you.

In moments of deep depression, when darkness feels unrelenting, know that He can shine a light of hope into your soul, Whisper truth into your mind: tell you that you are fearfully and wonderfully made (Psalm 139:14), you are deeply loved, and you have a purpose in life.

In times of mania, when you feel restless, overwhelmed, or out of control, know that He can bring calming peace with His hand on your life. He brings balance even when it feels impossible. Let Him hold you fast, hold you tight.

On this journey, there will be many moments when it feels heavy, but in those times, you are never forsaken. Even in our weakness, He is strong, His grace is always enough. Wrap yourself in His love.

I pray for your healing—whether through medication, therapy, or the touch of the Master's hand. Most of all, I pray for your peace.

Your illness does not define you. You have a purpose, and you are deeply loved. Bipolar disorder is a giant, but it is NOT bigger than God.

Thank you for joining me on this journey through *Fighting Goliath: Slaying the Giant of Bipolar Disorder.*

May you find peace knowing that God is with you on this journey and that you are never alone.

To the reader who does not know Jesus:
I want to take a moment to speak to you directly from a place of love. If you are reading this, you may be the one living with bipolar disorder or you may be facing another giant altogether. Maybe you are searching for your purpose—the peace that you long to find. I am not promising you a pain-free life. "Come to Me, all you who are weary and burdened, and I will give you rest" (Matthew 11:28). I promise someone to walk with you through your journey—one who

can provide a love that never fades or fails. If you are ready, all you need to do is ask Him to come into your life to help and guide you on this journey. If you accept His invitation, please let me know so we can celebrate this together! I encourage you to keep seeking, asking, and knocking if unsure. He is ready and willing to meet you exactly where you are.

My deepest gratitude,

Jesslyn

RESOURCES

988 Suicide & Crisis Lifeline
> Call or text 988, or chat at https://988lifeline.org/ to be connected to a trained crisis counselor. Deaf and Hard of Hearing call 711, then 988. Veterans call 988, then press 1 or text and word to 838255.

SAMHSA's National Helpline
> 1-800-662-HELP (4357)
> https://www.samhsa.gov/

NAMI National Helpline
> Mon–Fri, 10:00 a.m.-10:00 p.m. EST
> 800-950-NAMI (6264)
> Email: helpline@nami.org
> https://www.nami.org/help
> Text "helpline" to 62640, or chat online

NAMI Teen Young Adult Helpline
> Text "Friend" to 62640
> 1-800-950-NAMI (6264)
> https://www.nami.org/talktous

Depression and Bipolar Support Alliance (DBSA)
> (312) 642-0049
> https://www.dbsalliance.org/

International Bipolar Foundation
> 858-598-5967
> https://ibpf.org/
> Text "Connect" to 741741

The International OCD Foundation
    617-973-5801
    https://iocdf.org/

The National Center for PTSD
    https://www.ptsd.va.gov/

Veterans Crisis Line
    800-273-8255
    Text 838255
    Online chat at https://www.veteranscrisisline.net/

American Foundation for Suicide Prevention
    https://afsp.org

To find a warmline in your area and local mental health services:
    Dial 211
    https://www.211.org/